ALL BY GRACE

My Life in 5 Acts

by Rosie Howard

ISBN 978-1-98-301174-0

Front Cover: dawn-dusk-jetty-7196, copyright
free for private or commercial use
from pexels.com

Foreword

I have been blessed by many friends, most of whom know that I am a Christian. What they don't know is how I became a Christian, and why I hold the beliefs that I do. My intention, therefore, in writing this account of my life, is to address these two issues. When I was a child, almost every child was 'christened', went to Sunday School and, after a period of instruction, was 'confirmed' by a bishop through the laying on of hands in a service known as 'Confirmation'.

In modern society these steps cannot be assumed: many children could grow to adulthood with no input from the Church at all. They may not know who Jesus is, or why He died; indeed, they may not know of, let alone understand or seek to put into practice, the basic tenets of the Christian faith. My purpose, therefore, in writing this book is to set out through the circumstances of my life, how and why I became a Christian, and what being a Christian means to me.

If you are able to extract just one crumb from it and apply it in your own life, I will be very pleased. My intention has been to follow a chronological path as I have recounted the steps along my spiritual journey, though clearly some events are interwoven with others, so it is not set out in a strict chronology. I have added anecdotal material just to give depth and context to events as they unfolded. I hope they add rather than detract from the narrative. It has been both enjoyable and cathartic for me to write in this way, giving me a much greater understanding of the events and circumstances which formed my behaviour and beliefs.

I would like to express my very warm thanks to my husband Ian for his unfailing support and encouragement in the writing of this account of my life. I would also like to extend my very sincere thanks Dr Alison MacDonald, my 'Oxford' tutor in Archaeology, and Father Patrick, my tutor in Orthodox Christian Studies, both of whom have read the typescript and made very helpful suggestions. To Ian, Alison and Father Patrick, therefore, I am deeply indebted, and it is to them that I dedicate this book.

Rosie Howard

Carterton, Oxon. 2018

Contents Page

Act 5: 2016-18

Act 1

1945-1962

Chapter 1 : The Early Years

Our playroom, as I recall, was in the basement, whence a short flight of steps led up to the front door. A safety device was in place, installed by my parents, which prevented us from actually reaching the door; it could only be accessed by another stairway, out of our sight. But this is nonetheless my earliest recollection. I would be no older than two because we moved from this great Victorian behemoth of a house, ranged over five floors, two days before my third birthday. It was not the most convenient situation for a family of four young daughters, all under ten, with the 'bathroom', crude as it was, housed inside the turret on the fifth floor; but my parents were just so pleased that the War was over and they could be together again. My father, though a trained artist, had qualified as a Civil Engineer by attending evening classes and, when the War broke out, he was working for Portsmouth City Council. We were evacuated to Littlehampton and I was born in Rustington, in Sussex, but my father spent many days and nights during the War in Portsmouth, battling to protect that beleaguered city and its vulnerable inhabitants.

The house was rented and not our own. It had been requisitioned by the military during the War and my sisters tell me of the socks found in the boiler, or the great flitches of meat apparently thrown out of the window and into the back garden. Such behaviour naturally attracted vermin and my mother would recall the nights she spent with me as a baby only a few months old, in front of the embers of the fire, keeping me awake so that my asthma would not take me in the night. And while we sat, we watched the rats playing round her feet, in the warmth and light of that fire. And so the months passed and, unknown to me, my father had purchased a plot of land on the north-facing slopes of a local hill, and himself designed the house that he intended to build there.

He persevered in his endeavours, saw his plans come to fruition and, two days before my third birthday, on 3rd February 1948, we moved in. Post-war restrictions on building materials were still in place, and so he designed it in such a way that, when these restrictions were lifted, a study could be built on the ground floor and a fourth bedroom added upstairs. On a clear day we could see Butser Hill from our dining room window. The move to the hill had been suggested by our family doctor as a way of easing my wheezes. 'Otherwise', he said, 'you'll have to take the child to Switzerland'.

The year of 1948 was spent settling into this red-brick house and establishing the sloping gardens. My parents took great pleasure in planting bushes of soft fruit and fruit trees, as well as herbaceous borders, lawns and flowers, and a medium-sized vegetable patch. I can still picture the honeysuckle which we trained to grow through the chicken-wire fence, to create a less permeable barrier between us and our rather odd neighbours. I can remember the Michaelmas daisies which always blossomed on cue, and the blue-ish hydrangea and Rose of Sharon bushes which bordered the steps up to the front door. I can picture the coal store behind the corrugated iron shed, where we kept our bikes and where one of my sisters kept white mice until I, in my innocence, and taking pity on them in their captivity, let them out of their cage.

Sometimes, in the summer, my sisters and I would climb from the coal heap on to the roof of the shed and observe the long northward view which led to the South Downs. In the foreground, and not more than a mile or two from our house, was Southwick House, in which the Allied Naval Headquarters had been based during the Second World War. The corrugated iron would become very hot in the heat of the sun, and sometimes red ants would swarm over it and us, making our bare arms and legs itch and sting. That place on the roof, as well as the den we built at the bottom of the front garden, by the damson tree, became places of refuge for us, when we wanted to escape from any tensions in the house, or when we wanted to spy on our neighbours.

In my mind I can still take the short walk we took most Saturday mornings to buy pansies or nasturtiums for sixpence a-piece from the local nurseries, to bring back and plant in 'our' gardens. I can still taste the sweetness of the plums and damsons, redcurrants and the blackcurrants, the strawberries and the gooseberries; and experience again the joy of picking apples and eating them or mixing the 'cookers' with locally garnered blackberries in some delicious pudding. I distinguished myself by partially eating a worm, and a bush of fragrant rosemary was planted in 'my' garden. I was often unwell with my wheezes and recurring chest infections, and it was a time of rejoicing for me, throughout my childhood and into my teens that, once the acute phase had passed, I was allowed into the garden to breathe the fresh air and draw comfort from its planting. Usually I could only last a few minutes before the residual weakness in my body demanded a more comfortable seat than that afforded by the rustic bench which sat outside the living room window, but I was always pleased to spend even a short time in that lovely environment.

We cut the lawns ourselves, with two bad-tempered, mechanical, mowers; one heavy, with rollers and a 'hood', and the other lighter, with its rotating blades. I was spared the rota which dictated whose turn it was to cut the grass until I was older and stronger, but we always complained, muttering that the machines had not been cleaned or oiled since their last use. A man was employed to keep the grass on 'the slope' short: it was too steep and tricky for us. Only later did I discover that he was a gypsy, from a nearby camp, who had worked with my father on Civil Defence projects during the War. When, many years later, we sold the house, it was the gardens that I was most reluctant to leave.

Some time after my third birthday my father suggested that we, he and I, go the Post Office to buy me a paint-box. I felt so proud walking along beside him, hoping he couldn't see how hard my legs were having to work to keep up with him, nor how breathless I became with such exertion. He was always irreproachably dressed, with his suit and waistcoat, his gold fob watch on its gold chain, his detachable collar, perfectly starched and ironed, his trilby hat, his gloves, and his walking cane, which he swung up with one step and brought down to the ground, with a tap, with the next. Once in the Post Office he discussed the relative advantages and drawbacks of the various types of paint-box, and yet, very patiently, let me make my own decision.

Another memory that I cherish is that of him coming home from work and slumping in his favourite armchair, near the fire. He would balance his cup of tea precariously on its arm, and I was allowed to sit on his lap so long as I didn't move. I made sure during those precious moments that I stayed absolutely still. I'm sure he could be annoying: he chewed his food twenty times and never, as far as I'm aware, did any kind of housework.

Silly children annoyed him, and he would place the desire for a new lens for his camera above the (more legitimate, one might well say) call for expenditure on domestic or familial utility; so said my mother, with a calm acceptance born of experience. But we never went short because of it, and I loved him without reservation.

And so 1948 passed. My father ordered and took delivery of a car. We attended the nearby church and made friends locally and had every reason to believe that we could look forward to an ordered and peaceful future. My wheezes didn't improve (indeed, I suspect that all the detritus of the new-build probably aggravated my condition), but no more was said of Switzerland. The National Health Service was now established, and our local family doctor was assiduous in supporting me through my many illnesses. Summer turned to autumn and then to winter, and with it the enjoyment of our first Christmas in our new home. New Year followed and, although we didn't celebrate this together as a family, I was conscious that my parents were celebrating with friends downstairs, and that they were later than usual coming to bed. At this point my recollection is a little blurred.

I believe that I heard some unusual bumps and thumps in the night, with raised voices, but this may be a later construction.

Certainly in the morning things seemed to be different. People were acting strangely, relating to each other in an odd way. There were strangers in the home and the atmosphere was unusually quiet. This state of affairs lasted for two days and on the third day, the 3rd January 1949, it was my sister's birthday. And I realise, at this point, how remiss it is of me that I have got well into my story without introducing you to my family, so let me make amends. They have asked me to respect their privacy, and so I will only refer to them in the most general terms.

My father was tall and well-built, with a tendency to put on weight, particularly as war-time restrictions on food were lifted. He had a rounded but rectangular face, with a high forehead, full lips, a broad smile, and green eyes that were more penetrating than piercing. I felt that he not only looked at people, but also into them, weighing them up and judging them, but also esteeming them. He enjoyed, and I believe was good at, painting and photography; and loved old buildings, maps, plans and books, and antiques of all kinds. He amassed a collection of books, stamps and coins during the War, which is still in the possession of our family. His forbears had come from the Midlands and the north of England, but his mother was insistent that the family 'had come over with William the Conqueror'. I would ask him why he would say 'bath' and 'grass' with a short 'a', while I said 'baath' and 'graass', in the southern way. He said it was because he had been brought up in a different part of the country.

My mother, though coming from North London, was definitely 'foreign' – with her inky-black straight hair and olive skin, her high and wide cheekbones, her straight and fine nose and her hetero-chromatic (one blue and one green) eyes. Her mother had been a German immigrant who came to England when she was eighteen, in the 1890s. She, my mother, was tall and striking and, when younger, had had her hair cut in a fashionable 'Eton Crop'. She hated the time when her very dark hair began to go white, badger-like, in a V over her left eye-brow, and would try to conceal it with shoe-polish. She was a wise and loving wife and mother, as well as being an excellent cook and a gifted home-maker.

I loved both my parents, but to me my mother was the bread-and-butter, while my father, with his high standards and autocratic ways, was the icing on the cake. They had met at a tea-dance in London, when he was living and working in Wandsworth, and had married in 1932.

They had four daughters, of which I was the youngest. My oldest sister was nine years older than I. She was shorter than the rest of us and left home to train as a nurse when she was seventeen. Though very able, she suffered throughout her life from bouts of depression, which deeply affected her and all the family. She never married and, having converted to Catholicism, she died 12 years ago. My next sister was six years older than I. She became a teacher, was married, and had two daughters. The third sister was just under two years older than I. She became a teacher and university lecturer; she is married and has a daughter. I was born just before the end of the War in February 1945, and was christened Rosemarie Maude, the Marie being taken from my maternal (German) grandmother, and Maude taken from my aunt. I'm sure they had hoped for a boy, but the family had to wait for over forty years before another son entered its ranks, when my own son was born, the first in the family for almost 70 years. I also have a daughter. As you can see, it was a very female-orientated family, with only my father representing the male line. But we must now return to these 'odd' post-New-Year days.

It was my second sister's tenth birthday on 3rd January and, as usual, my mother had prepared (and God only knows how), a 'proper' birthday tea. As we sat around the dining table I noticed that my father wasn't there. My mother was sitting next to me and so I asked her where he was.

She looked at me for a moment and then told me that he had gone away and wouldn't be coming back. 'What have you done with him?', was the only question on my mind. Why would he go away on my sister's birthday and miss the party? And where had he gone? I presumed it couldn't be far, but there was something very bad going on. Gradually the realisation dawned that he had gone to a place where I couldn't follow. That he had died. And those bumps and thumps I had heard in the night were the desperate attempts made, both by my mother and by the doctor who lived across the road, to revive him. But there was nothing to be done. Having celebrated the New Year rather well, he suffered a coronary thrombosis and died before morning. He was 41, and we later discovered that he'd had a 'heart murmur'. The 'strangeness' I had felt in those early days was presumably the adult reaction to the shock and grief they felt as he lay cold upon the bed upstairs.

For me it was terrible news, more dreadful than I could possibly have imagined I had loved him with a passion and now he was gone. It was he, I thought, who gave us status and dignity in society. He who would provide for us and protect us. When he was with me I felt strong and happy. I loved his special clothes and his old-fashioned ways. I loved the fact that he allowed me into his dark room in 'the loft' (that is, the attic) where, with string slung from beams, he hung up his photographs to dry; or where he poured water from a large old black kettle into shallow developing trays and, as if by magic, images gradually appeared.

I loved the side of his head, from his temple to his jaw, passed his ear, which my mother traversed with hair clippers when she trimmed his hair in the kitchen. I wanted to run my finger along the soft skin by his hairline, but I knew that that would be out of place. This was their little ritual, as a couple, and I was there only as a privileged observer. I loved the little suitcase he took to work, containing a newspaper and his lunch, which he clasped as he ran the short distance down the lane to the bus-stop. I have it still. As I recalled these and other memories I was flooded with grief. How was I going to live without him? How would we manage without him? It was as though my life, as I knew it, was over. As though someone had flicked a dimmer switch and suddenly life was darker and sadder than I could possibly imagine.

Chapter 2 : Dealing with Grief

Before he died, my father and mother had been strong and wise leaders of our rather volatile family, intervening with authority if sisterly spats became too heated, and somehow finding personal time for each of us in the course of their busy lives, most particularly at bedtimes. But after my father had gone my mother seemed more vulnerable and we exploited that, both in our relationship with her, and with each other. It has always been a trait of mine, whether a weakness or a strength I cannot say, that rules for various activities, whether work, play or sport, should be established between the various parties involved, and then adhered to. It always spurred me to anger, and sometimes uncontrollable anger, when rules were bent or discarded, for whatever reason, though usually in the overwhelming desire to 'win'.

One such incident occurred when my sisters and I were playing. I cannot remember the details, and I was only quite young, but someone said or did something which caused me to erupt. In my fury I picked up the heavy poker which lay on the hearth, and swung it over one of my sisters, intending to hit her on the head. With great presence of mind she ducked and so avoided injury, the poker coming down instead on one of my mother's favourite Doulton pots. I was beside myself. I felt that I had been set up, and knew that I would be punished. When my mother heard our angry cries and came in from the kitchen, she saw me with the raised poker, and the damaged pot, and reacted exactly as I had predicted. I was taken to my room, and told to stay there until she called me down.

I raved and objected, but there was nothing to be done, and I stayed on my bed, nursing my injured pride and sniffling with anger, until sometime later when I was allowed down. But when we went to bed that night she found time to talk to me on my own, sitting on the bed and holding my hands in her lap. Did she understand, I wondered? Could she see that I had been set up? Was there anyone, anywhere, I wondered, who knew everything and could 'judge' events accurately and impartially? As she sat there she told me that I must learn to control my temper; that my sisters would provoke me endlessly while they knew just how I would react. But if I didn't react, then in time, said my mother, they would stop provoking me. And so it turned out. From that day on I resolved to conceal my emotions: that I would be cool and aloof, not allowing people or circumstances to penetrate my protective outer layer. It was a policy which I adopted and applied, with varying degrees of success, well until my mid-thirties, until another and better way was shown me.

Somehow we got through those early days, but when one of the dinner ladies at school said she was sorry to hear that my father had died, I would have none of it. 'Oh no', I said', 'he hasn't died'. I didn't want sympathy or compassion from someone I didn't know very well. While I denied such expressions of sympathy, I thought, there was a chance that he might come back, that he wasn't really dead at all. And so the grief went deeper into some internal chamber, where it lingered and festered, weighing on me and distressing me, particularly at night, in bed, with the light out. Sometimes, when the pain of it all was almost too great to bear, I would ask my mother if she would make me a 'surprise' for the morning. This was our little code. But it worked for, in the morning, and from the scraps in her sewing basket, there would be on my bedside table a simple soft toy, or a small bag, or a quickly-embroidered bookmark.

These helped enormously, bringing comfort and pleasure, but it would be many years before I found relief from this tragic burden; and if anything went wrong, in whatever quarter, either personally or externally, I would blame it on the loss of my father.

One incident stands out in my memory from those early days of grief which has remained with me. For some reason, one night, I was conscious that my mother had not come up to bed. Noting that the sister with whom I shared a room was asleep, I slipped out of bed, crossed the landing, went down the stairs - passed the lovely long window which in daytime illuminated them - and continued through the dining room to the living room, where I believed my mother to be. At first I could see very little, for there were no lights on, but gradually, as my eyes adjusted to the gloom, I saw her sitting down and outlined by the glow from the dying fire. I sat down with her and asked her what she was doing there, and why hadn't she gone to bed.

She said she had been thinking about things. What things, I asked, even though I knew there could be only one topic on her mind. How we are going to manage, she said. Apparently, well-meaning but ill-advised colleagues and relations wanted to put us children into a Home, and she would be found some employment. But no, she said, she felt that this was the path that God had set for her: that she must keep the family together in the home which had been built for us, and that God would provide for us. This was a shocking sentiment to me. The God I had come to know from Sunday School was remote but kindly, like an affable uncle; I couldn't imagine a God who would require such courage and submission. I stayed quietly with her for a while and then went back to bed, and she followed soon after.

At that time I had no idea of the financial

implications of what she was proposing. As time went on I understood that she received a Widow's Pension from the State, as well as benefit both from NALGO, (National Association of Local Government Officers), and from the Institute of Chartered Civil Engineers, who also sent us a hamper of food at Christmas. But times were often very hard; the small mortgage on the house was not covered by insurance, and the finances needed very careful management. I, as the youngest, was used to hand-me-downs, and tried not to complain, but I did love it when we went shopping for clothes, my mother and I, just for me. It was a particular outfitter we had to use for our school uniform and, once the garment had been chosen, it would be wrapped in tissue paper and placed in a cardboard box with a lid, and the whole would be tied with cotton tape. I loved the speed and dexterity with which the assistant accomplished these tasks, and almost more magical, to me at least, was the way in which we paid for them.

For an invoice would be written and coupons handed over, if necessary, as well as the cash. These then would be placed in a canister which, as if by magic, would suddenly – with a rattling and whooshing sound – be sucked away to some nether region where, presumably, a cashier would complete the transaction. There was no knowing how long this process would take and so we stood around making small-talk but all the time, at the back of my mind at least, waiting with heightened anticipation for the unmistakable whizzing and rattling which would herald the return of the canister, with a receipt and any change that was owed. I would emerge from the shop beaming and replete, having enjoyed the whole glorious event, and looked forward to some refreshment in a nearby teahouse, to make my joy complete.

Another source of predictable pleasure for me was the visits we would make to the old-fashioned grocer's shop in our local town. For here groceries of all kinds – butter, biscuits, and sugar come to mind – were displayed in their various cabinets, or jars, or on shelves; and each purchase was accompanied by a little ritual. Broken biscuits and sugar would be packaged in swiftly-made cones of blue sugar-paper; butter would be cut from a large block kept cool on a marble slab, and then beaten into a rectangular shape with two wooden 'paddles', before being stamped and neatly wrapped in greaseproof paper. Other items had similar associated actions, and all the while a genuine, if light, conversation would be conducted between my mother and the proprietor. In truth we only bought a few items in the shop; my mother didn't drive and we couldn't carry a lot.

In any case, the tradition seemed to be that a middle-aged representative of the grocery shop would call on us once a week and she, sitting in the kitchen and enjoying a cup of tea, would take our order, which would then be delivered by van a few days later.

Some goods were sold at the back-door: the fishmonger came on Fridays, the baker came more frequently, as did the greengrocer, whose clever van had fold-up sides which revealed banks of fresh fruit and vegetables. Meat was bought from the butcher in the village, where an Oxo cube could be bought by us children for a farthing. Tradesmen were central to our lives and we knew them all, even the coal-men, whose sacks my sister and I counted closely from the security of our 'den', as they were carried, gnome-like, up the front path to the coal heap, making sure that they didn't sell us short. It was a terrible shock to me therefore when, not long after, supermarkets were opened; with their cold fluorescent lighting and disembodied music and bland pre-packaged produce and a bored assistant waiting at the check-out. I longed for, and still do, the essential human interaction which made these earlier shopping events so enjoyable.

These post-War times were hard, not just for us but also for the many families who had lost their breadwinners. Yet somehow we managed; extraordinarily - on one occasion - finding a £5 note stuck in the hedge outside our kitchen door, which paid for the weekend joint and other groceries. My mother was a remarkable woman, and demonstrated both tenacity and courage during those sad and difficult times; and she made good on the commitment which she had shared with me during that distant night-time encounter. By her efforts and the grace of God we were able to stay together as a family, and to live in the home that our father had built for us.

She hadn't been raised as a Christian. Her mother, distraught after the loss of her eldest son, had had her baptised into a London Spiritualist Church, but I don't think she attended any of their meetings. She, like her mother before her, could 'read' our hands, and 'interpret' tea-leaf formations at the bottom of cups, but these were just games we played with her as children. Later, in adulthood, and as my own Christian faith developed, I felt I should (and did) repent of those times, recognising them as occult activities. My father, on the other hand, had been raised in a Christian family and had a deep faith of his own. Because of him we went to church and Sunday School, and he taught us to recite simple Christian poems, and to say, 'The Lord's Prayer' as we knelt beside the bed.

And in the weeks following his death my mother had the strong conviction that she should be confirmed in the Anglican Church, which she did, submitting herself to a course of instruction and having episcopal hands laid upon her.

In Sunday School I sang, 'This little guiding light

of mine, I'm going to let it shine', holding up the index finger of my right hand and waving it around. 'Hide it under a bush, oh no!', I sang heartily, momentarily covering it with my left hand and then dramatically removing it. I just loved the tune and the actions; I didn't yet understand the Christian faith, but I knew that my father had believed it and, in his absence, wanted to honour him by following it in the ways that I could. In the course of 1948 he had gone away on a residential course for some reason - whether as a Civil Engineer or as a lecturer in photography which he had also now become, I don't know - and I must have sent him a 'letter', with scribbles and illustrations. To my joy he responded with a proper, hand-written, letter, also illustrated, in which he observed, among other things, that, 'there aren't many little girls around here.' I was so pleased and treasured that letter, which I still have.

My attendance at school caused me very real anxiety and unhappiness. Why did I have to leave the security and comfort of my own home and go to what I considered to be a hostile and overly- competitive environment?

At home I could sit by the fire and look at my books, or accompany my mother to the Sewing Bee held in the local Church Hall. I could talk to people who treated me kindly and drink cups of tea with them. Indeed, when my mother hosted what was known as the 'Prayer Cell' at home, I would drink tea from my favourite white cuboid tea-pot and enrich it with five teaspoons of sugar. It was subsequently only when I was ill (and I was ill quite a lot with a condition known as 'bronchial-asthma'), that I was able to indulge these excesses. Otherwise school made its entirely legitimate demands on my life and I had to knuckle under.

The 11+ exam loomed large and I, not really understanding what was required of me, failed it. It was a horrible feeling, but in fact the two years which I spent at the co-educational Secondary Modern School were rather happy and successful. I passed the 13+ exam and went to the local Grammar School, with my next sister. By this time I was conscious of the physical changes taking place in my body. My hair, normally lustrous and only slightly wavy, became greasy and frizzy. My nose grew bigger and my skin was subject to incipient acne. I was tall and well-developed for my age and wore glasses and hated the brown beret I was required to wear as part of the uniform. Why couldn't I be like some of my friends, I wondered, with their straight fringes and pert turned-up noses, their swinging pony-tails and smooth skins, their muscular legs, tiny waists and slender athletic bodies?

But help was at hand for that spring, when I was twelve and recovering from a severe bout of 'bronchial-pneumonia', my mother knitted me

- with large wooden needles and chunky wool - a vast blue jumper called a 'Sloppy Jo'. It was wonderful! I felt it completely covered my troublesome torso and I could allow my metamorphosis to take place out of sight, rather like a moth in its cocoon. It took me weeks to recover from the debilitating effects of that illness, particularly as, at that time, there was very little that could be done for asthma, and antibiotics were in their infancy. It was at times such as this that I developed my love of reading, borrowing books from my sisters' shelves and the local public library, as well as building up a respectable collection of my own. Enid Blyton, Malcolm Saville, Monica Edwards and Ruby Ferguson were favourite authors, as well as John Buchan and M. Pardoe and her wonderful 'Bunkle' series, most of which I still own. I also started writing, mostly short stories and probably not very good ones; but they helped me to pass the dreadful days and nights of fever and wheezing.

At that time my older sisters would spend, in my view, very exciting days in London, listening to Billy Graham as he led rallies at White City and Harringay. They were deeply impressed by him, and I noticed that one of my sisters would sit on the bed and read her Bible, leaving the door open so that we younger siblings could be stirred to emulation by her example. I felt bad when I found it annoying. But there was no doubt that Billy Graham, and others, were having a powerful influence in the Church, with their simple message of repentance and belief, and I wished them well. They would also go, on Saturday nights, to a club called the *Pomme d'Or*. I had no idea what that was and thought it was some particular kind of door; and I would watch them closely as they put on special clothes and applied make-up and carefully did their hair. Some part of me said it was all wicked; that no good would come of it, and they should just stay at home and listen to the radio and do their knitting with the rest of the family.

Only later did I understand that it was a place of jiving and rock-and-roll, and that the radio, and knitting, could in no way compete with this new craze from America. I had also seen (from the top of the bus) 'teddy-boys' standing on street corners, displaying their knuckle-dusters and grooming their quiffs, and I thought that they, too, were a bad and dangerous new element in society. I wanted certainty and the old order, and preferred to pursue, at least at that time, more traditional activities.

One of these was the passion I developed for horse-riding during my early teens. There was a rather modest riding school not far from our home, to which one of my sisters and I would cycle on Saturday mornings, and spend many happy hours cleaning the tack, catching and saddling up the ponies, and then going for a ride. I especially loved the soap which we used to soften, clean and polish the saddles. From a jumble sale I acquired a pair of Land Army breeches, with laces at the sides, which I wore with long socks and lace-up shoes. Later I was able to buy a proper pair of jodhpurs and they, with my velvety hard hat and riding crop, made me feel very professional. I did have a tweed jacket, but it was also a jumble sale find and not a 'proper' hacking jacket. I think I liked the clothes as much as the horses. I wasn't particularly athletic; I sometimes fell off and never competed at events, but it is a phase of my life which I look back on with great affection.

It was during this time, when I was in my teens, that I started to understand more about the Christian faith. We studied Religious Instruction as part of our preparation for 'O' Levels and that, combined with the teaching I received at church, gave me a limited understanding of the New Testament and the life of Jesus. I believed in God, but my theology was a little confused and I didn't understand what it meant to live out one's faith. 'Try to do your best and follow the example of Jesus', could sum up my approach, but it was an ill-formed doctrine which I put into practice with limited success.

But I became an accomplished churchgoer, able to recite large chunks of the Book of Common Prayer by heart. I could navigate my way around the Bible, and frequently read the Lesson in church. I knew most of the most popular hymns and could sing the Psalms; I felt at home in the church building and was familiar with the choreography of the different services. In hindsight I can see that the theology of my church at that time was 'liberal/Catholic'; while being friendly and inclusive, it didn't really teach or stress the importance of personal salvation and the new birth.

I did pray, and I did the best that I could, but forces were already at work which would completely undermine my tender faith. One of those was a book written by the Revd Dr John Robinson called 'Honest to God', which seemed to imply that one could create one's own gospel. That it was all right to admit to doubt and disbelief, so long as one was honest. For a mature and robust faith this would not have been much of a problem. For me, with my limited theological understanding, it was a death-knell. Another factor was that my 'next' sister was leaving home to attend Teacher Training College in London. She had always guided and supported me, and I didn't know how I would cope without her strong presence. Now, like a ship becalmed in the doldrums, I felt rudderless and directionless.

Our local vicar was 'promoted' and moved to the Midlands: he had been a family friend and had made us feel valued in the life of the church. Under his leadership we had been members of the Sunday School, Brownies and Guides, and then sung in the choir. With his children we had been active in the CYF (Church Youth Fellowship). Through him and his family we had felt a very strong connection to, and ease with, the activities of the church. My mother was a close friend of his wife and they ran the 'Prayer Cell' together; and, through a 'secret' pathway between the back-gardens, we were frequent visitors to each other's homes.

His replacement was quite a different kind of person, and we didn't relate to him at all in the same way. Suddenly our family home, once so full of bustle and activity, was almost empty and my mother took a job as a secretary in a local office. Nothing was the same any more, and I couldn't cope with the change. I could feel my faith, fragile as it already was, being eroded, and it would only take another blow for it to implode all together. And this blow came from an unexpected source.

For, over the preceding months, I had been befriended by a youth worker who was attached both to our church and to the local Scout group, and who had helped me to understand the rudiments of the Christian faith. He told me that he had been accused, quite unjustly he insisted, of relating inappropriately with Scouts in the course of his duties. I sympathised, and prayed, with him. However, some weeks later when his case finally came to court, he admitted the charges that had been brought and asked for a large number of other cases, previously unknown, to be taken into consideration. It was a terrible blow. I had trusted him and felt betrayed. More than that, my faith was in tatters. I tried to pray, but nothing 'came'. I tried to read the Bible, but it made no sense to me. It was like trying to press a button where the power had been discontinued: I was going through the process of 'believing' but in reality I felt that there was nothing there. I was in my late teens and at that stage, even though I didn't know it, I had entered into a time of estrangement from God, or a 'prodigal loop', which was to last for another seventeen years.

Two more things of importance took place in those momentous years; the first was inward and private, the second was public and obvious. The first was the decision I took, without any external pressure, to draw a line under my loss of faith and the years of unresolved grief. I felt that I should take responsibility for my own actions, and not blame my shortcomings or failures on the God I no longer believed in, or on the loss of my father. These were big decisions, I thought, but even if I hadn't resolved the issue of my grief, I could no longer use it as an excuse for not accomplishing things.

I have the image in my mind of actually drawing a thick line in pencil in my diary: this may be a later construction of my memory, but I certainly recall the feelings of resolve and relief I experienced, when I had decided upon this.

The second was my decision to leave school. I had done reasonably well at 'O' Level and had embarked on my 'A' Levels, but I found them very stressful. Somehow more was required of me, with less guidance and support, and I felt vulnerable. The stress, of course, exacerbated my asthma which, in turn, weakened my immune system and caused me to suffer from increased infections. And these took their toll on my work, for each 'bout' would take me out of school for three weeks, and then I was 'wobbly' and not sufficiently recovered to pick up the reins of academic work again, let alone catch up on all that I had missed. As a consequence, at the end of the Lower Sixth, I was given a large dossier of work to do over the summer holiday, which involved not only reading books, but also writing essays. But the holidays came and went and I did none of the tasks set me. It was only as the days before my return dawned that I realised the horrible consequences of my inaction.

My teachers were literally of the old school, exacting, short on praise and high on criticism, and I simply could not face their inevitably angry and frustrated reaction when I sought to explain myself. My mother was sad but not cross. She tried to dissuade me, but I would not budge. Better the sadness than the humiliation, I thought and, with the stubbornness which I could display when it suited me, I insisted on leaving. Inwardly I was frightened by my actions, but I tried not to let that show. I would easily get a job, I thought, and earn some money, and buy some clothes and make-up, and get my hair cut in a new and fashionable way. The 'Swinging Sixties' were still in their infancy, but there was definitely a new *Zeitgeist* abroad, with a powerful drumbeat which seemed to beckon me. And so the die was cast and I set off to find a job.

Act 2

1962-1979

Chapter 3 : Into the Unknown

I thought it would be easy, finding a job, but in fact it proved to be rather difficult. It appeared that I was under-qualified for some jobs, the more interesting ones, and over-qualified for others. In the end I secured a position as a clerk in the Bought Ledger section of a local firm of builders' merchants. To begin I had to master some very simple and repetitive tasks, but quite soon I got the measure of things and was promoted to the operating of a great clattering machine, which not only produced details of goods 'bought', mechanically and according to my typed instructions; but also printed out cheques, which then had to be signed. The skill was in making sure that all the amounts tallied at the end of the day, otherwise one simply had to stay until the error was found and rectified. I rather liked the complexity and responsibility of that job. I was eighteen and earned £4.50 a week, in cash, after deductions.

I observed with interest the people with whom I worked, the sort of people I had never, in my secluded existence, met before. Sailors' wives and girlfriends predominated, and I listened with round-eyed amazement as life at sea, and on land, was regaled. It was during this time that I began to smoke cigarettes, in emulation of these colleagues and to the dismay of my gentle mother who was thinking, no doubt, as much of the deleterious effect on my lungs as of the pollution I caused around the home. And of the cost in relation to my pay. I didn't care: I had to be *à la mode* in relation to my working colleagues; I thought I looked 'cool', and it helped me to lose weight.

It became clear to me, after some months, that – although I found this particular job interesting – working at this level as a career would not satisfy me, and so I enrolled at the local Technical College to do a full-time two-year Diploma in Business Studies. It was right to move on, but the experience I gained from that time was not wasted. It gave me my first insight into the world of 'work', and of 'business'; and when, at the end of my Diploma, I had to write a dissertation on some aspect of 'business-management', it served as my model. While at College I became active in the Students' Union, putatively to give expression to my (then) rather left-wing views; in reality it was in the hope of meeting a potential husband. Ever since I had turned sixteen I had been acutely aware of being 'a spinster of this parish' and wanted to rectify that as soon as possible. I couldn't be particularly discerning, I felt: that, as the none-too-beautiful youngest daughter of a practically-penniless widow, I had little to commend me in the marriage market.

Therefore, when I met a young physicist who was also involved with the Students' Union, and who shared my political views and, wanted to move to and work in London, I was very pleased to nurture the relationship. His parents were on active service overseas, and he lived with his grandmother. We both wanted change and, in each other's company, found the courage and motivation to pursue it. We came from very different social backgrounds, but I didn't see that as a problem. In a very short space of time, therefore, and with the minimum of expenditure and fuss, we were married and moved to London. He was a week older than I, and we were both twenty-one. Our wedding day was 29th July 1966, the significance of which escaped me at the time, but it was deliberately planned as the day before England played in the Final of the World Cup and which, against all the odds, won. It was an auspicious beginning to my new married life.

For the first two years we were surprisingly happy. We lived in rented accommodation, first in Balham and then in East Putney. I gave up smoking and worked in the Marketing Department of a large multi-national oil company, where I seemed to be doing rather well. My husband worked as a research scientist at London University, in Kensington. There was a spirit of permissiveness in the air, which meant that my skirts got shorter, and my make-up more exaggerated and my hair more *bouffant*, particularly when augmented with various ill-applied hairpieces.

The 'pill' meant there was no risk of an unwanted pregnancy. I could dance, and wear clothes and accessories well, and discovered that, when I abandoned my 'John Lennon' spectacles for newly-invented and very uncomfortable contact lenses, my face was rather attractive. That made a huge difference to my self-esteem. We enjoyed the proximity to central London, with its burgeoning attractions, but we also enjoyed more mundane and local pursuits, such as our habit of walking down to Putney High Street on Saturday mornings, browsing through the shops and stopping to drink coffee.

On one such Saturday, and this would be in 1968, there was an unusual commotion in the High Street, which closer inspection revealed to be a march or demonstration of some kind. We enquired of an official what it was about and was told that it was in support of the withdrawal of British troops from Northern Ireland. Did we agree with such views, we were asked. Half-heartedly we said yes, not at all understanding the implications of the question, or what the real issues were. I noted that it was a well-ordered march, with 'properly' printed banners, all under the aegis of something called 'The Socialist Labour League'. Even as I write this, I can feel the fear and foreboding that that name came to exert over me. I took little notice of events at the time, but my husband must have passed on our address, for the man who had spoken to him came to visit us, I think that evening, but it may have been shortly after. I responded in the only way I knew, politely admitting him and offering refreshments. And so began, all unobtrusively and imperceptibly, a nightmare period in my life, which left me physically and mentally exhausted, and almost broken.

For this man was a senior member of 'The Socialist Workers Party', and his aim was to recruit my husband to 'The Cause', that is, the violent overthrow of Capitalism, the destruction of the hated *bourgeoisie*, the rise of the proletariat and the establishment of a truly egalitarian Marxist society. My study of Economics, and particularly of Economic History, made me very wary of the pursuit of such aims, but my husband seemed more than half-way convinced of their legitimacy; and our visitor, seeing the potential of a rift between us, exploited it to the full. If I asked a question I would be 'blanked' and the reply directed at my husband though, in the pattern of dialectics in which our Marxist had been trained, the 'reply' generally took the form of another question, the only logical response to which would pave the way for the next 'question'.

I became annoyed that my role as 'hostess' was being ignored, and asked him to leave and not come back, but he came back nonetheless, and my husband did nothing to dissuade him. Gradually my husband was invited to their headquarters for more dialectical discussion, and then invited to join the teams that demonstrated over various issues and at various locations throughout the country. I saw him less and less and was, in turn, both angry and sad. But he would not deny his new-found comrades and their radical views, and all my pleadings, and tears, would not avail. Eventually he was invited to join them on a weekend camp, and it was at this point that things went from bad to much worse.

When he went away he had a beard and his hair was fashionably long. He had dressed with an individual style, appropriate to the time and circumstances; he had enjoyed the songs of Bob Dylan, Leonard Cohen and Nina Simone and others of that genre; he had been gentle, easy-going and good company. On his return he seemed to be a different person. His hair was short and the beard had gone. He didn't smile or demonstrate, either in his speech or his body language, any kind of warmth or affection.

And perhaps the most shocking change that had taken place was in his eyes: they had been warm and humorous and engaging; now they were as cold and dull as pebbles, looking at me without any kind of spark or tenderness. I was instructed to sit and listen to him as he soaked in the bath, and was told that I had two choices. I could remain married to him if I agreed to submit to The Cause, as he had done; or I must, as a member of the despised middle classes, be broken. If I chose the former it would mean the complete loss of individualism - in style and expression - as well as in the use of my time and money. The marriage would only have legitimacy to the extent that it served the purposes of The Cause. If I chose the latter then I was a *persona non grata*, abandoned as useless and worse, a parasite.

It was a terrible dilemma. I had been happily married, I thought, and wanted the marriage to continue. Could I rescue him? For I could see that he had been brainwashed, in the mind-changing process that is now called radicalisation. Could love break through that barrier? For days I was weighed down with the enormity of my problem, and in the end I decided to remain with him and do what I could to enter his world. We kept our flat and I stayed in my job, but before work I had to sell the newspaper, *The Socialist Worker,* at factory gates; and after work I had to join teams going from door to door, spreading the gospel of Marxism and seeking to sell the newspaper and thereby recoup our losses, for each day we had to buy our 'quota'. After that it was a trawl through pubs and restaurants, followed by 'missionary' visits to coach- and railway-stations, before re-forming at the headquarters and being forced to engage in the hated dialectics.

I became so tired by that time, and longed for

my bed, but was horrified to find that, uninvited, various members of the Party would come home with us, dumping their unsold newspapers on our floors, eating our food and sleeping where they chose. My carefully managed home became a smelly tip, with unwashed pots and pans and the residual smell of unwashed bodies and clothes. There was just one aspect of this dreary routine that brought me any cheer. One of the factories I had to visit was based on Barnes Common, and I had to be there early in the morning to sell papers to the workers at the gates as they arrived. I can't recollect how I got to Barnes Common - it was probably by bus - but I do recall the rabbits and squirrels that were bounding around, going about their business as the dew lay heavily on the ground. They cheered me wonderfully and reminded me of a happier world outside the dark, cruel and grubby place that I was presently forced to inhabit.

I tried to maintain a level of normality in terms of my job, but it became obvious to those who knew me well that something serious was amiss. Apart from the strict prohibitions on individualism in terms of clothes, make-up and general appearance, I was constrained simply by exhaustion, not having the mental or physical energy to maintain the high standards in my personal life which had been so dear to me. I felt that my life was spiralling out of control and I could do nothing to prevent it. One colleague at work was especially watchful and kind, and always made sure that I had something substantial to eat for lunch. I told him a bit about my circumstances, but on the whole I kept the world at bay, including my family, regarding the changes that had happened. Despite it not being my fault, I nonetheless felt 'guilty'.

I believed deeply that marriage was for life, and couldn't contemplate for many months the prospect of separation, let alone divorce. I didn't want to put myself or my family through such shame and misery. Alongside the great chamber in my heart which contained the grief associated with the loss of my father, another room opened up, that containing the sadness, anger and disappointment I felt about the failure of this relationship. Soon, it seemed to me, and metaphorically-speaking, this room became full and threatened to explode, precipitating a deep crisis. I knew I had to act.

I therefore made the decision to stop 'serving' The Cause, knowing full well what the consequences of that decision would be. 'So be it', I thought, 'even if it leads to humiliation and disgrace, I cannot continue this course of action'. In turn I stopped selling newspapers at factory gates; I stopped going from door-to-door, or around pubs and restaurants, coach- and train-stations. I stopped attending rallies and demonstrations, I stopped engaging in futile dialectics and I stopped trying to 'save' my husband and my marriage. In my weariness and confusion I thought that any life would be better than the *danse macabre* I was performing, against both my will and my better judgement. Instead I caught up on lost sleep. I took trouble with my appearance; I read novels and met with friends for coffee. It was like emerging into warm sunshine after a long period of cold and darkness. But it did, as I knew, mean the end of my marriage. My husband put some of my belongings into the hallway of our flat and I was told when I could pick them up, which - helped by the kind colleague from work - I did one weekend when I believed him to be away. We never spoke again and only made contact through our solicitors as the divorce proceedings unfolded.

Just about that time a new Divorce Law had just been passed, which enabled me to divorce him on the grounds that, 'he was not reasonably fit to live with', the reinterpretation of the former 'mental cruelty' clause. The judge said it was the worst case he had ever heard, apart from one of extreme religious persecution. Some months later I saw my husband, though he didn't see me, as he went from door to door with a comrade on a housing estate, peddling dogma and newspapers. My heart slammed in my chest with fear, but I was able to hide, and then slip away unnoticed. Some years later I saw him from the top of a bus, now with grey hair and looking more like his former self. Perhaps even he, in time, had become disaffected? The marriage had lasted for four years, until 1970, when I was 25. I took a long and hard look at my life and wondered how I would react to being, and being treated as, a divorced woman. It was a shocking and sobering thought.

Chapter 4: A French Interlude

After the turbulence of the recent months I wanted nothing more than a safe space where I could recover and lick my wounds. I still had my job, and I had been able to rent a bed-sit in a large house, also in East Putney, where I had my own small kitchen (in a cupboard), but shared a bathroom. It had limited storage space, but I had few possessions and it suited me very well. I had never had a holiday as an adult and, apart from attending a Girl Guide camp in Jersey when I was twelve, I had never been out of the country. I shared these thoughts with my mother, and she agreed to explore the possibility of a 'package' holiday (which were then in their infancy) with a local travel agent. Her investigations proved to be productive, for she was recommended a holiday in the south of France, Nice, to be exact, run by the *Société Nationale des Chemins de Fer* (SNCF), that is, French National Railways. The price was inclusive and would cover the cost of the boat train to Paris and the sleeper from Paris to Nice, as well as ten days in Nice, with half-board, and then the return journey. It sounded ideal, and so it proved to be.

I loved the journey, especially the stretch from Paris to Nice, when the cheerful steward made up our bunks and settled us in for the night. In the morning, after a very good night's sleep, he brought us bowls of steaming coffee and rolls. By this time the sun was up and I could smell the 'hot' aroma of Provence which, when combined (strangely) with the 'hot' diesel fumes from the engine, I found quite intoxicating. I could have remained sitting in my seat, in seclusion and comfort, but I preferred to stand in the corridor, just so I could see better and inhale those blessed fumes. Finally, after a memorable stretch along the Mediterranean coast, we arrived, and a mini-bus took us seamlessly to our hotel.

We had separate rooms. My mother's room, with its high ceiling, French windows and balcony, was larger and located in the old original part of the hotel. My room, with its modern bathroom, was smaller, and was part of a more recent extension. I went to her room each morning and, on the internal phone, and in my best 'O' level French, ordered our breakfast. It was always the same (though sometimes she wanted a boiled egg as well), and never disappointed: piping hot coffee in a heavy silver pot, orange juice, *petits pains*, unsalted butter and apricot jam. I loved it. This was also my mother's first trip abroad, apart from her honeymoon in Guernsey; and she took her sketch pad and pencils with her, taking great delight in drawing the adjacent buildings, with their jumble of roofs and chimneys. I had my books with me, which were by now mostly Penguin paperbacks, and read voraciously.

Sometimes I got up very early and, before breakfast, went into the neighbouring streets, where the pavements were being washed, where the florists were busy setting out their flowers, and where there was an all-pervading smell of hot coffee and freshly-baked bread. After breakfast we would meet in the foyer, hand in our keys, and head for the Promenade, which was no more than three minutes' walk away. There we would hire deck chairs and settle ourselves in the sun. It was already warm and would soon be hot, but the breeze from the sea was very pleasant, and the time passed comfortably. My mother would buy filled baguettes for our lunch, with some beverage, which fortified us until mid-afternoon when, assuming that all necessary cleaning in our rooms had been done, we returned to our hotel, for rest and refreshment.

Later in the afternoon we would meet up again and go into the lovely old town of Nice, or wander in the beautiful 'Albert' gardens, or sometimes go even further afield. One day we took a tour to the nearby town of Grasse, one of the great centres of the perfume industry, and visited the venerable Fragonard factory, where my mother bought a presentation box of soap and *eau de toilette*.

In the early evening we would find a restaurant where the coupons issued by our hotel were accepted, and order our evening meal from a simple but filling and delicious menu. Sometimes we had a pizza for two, larger than any I had ever seen, with *a thin and crispy* base, (so different from the ones then found in England), laden with fresh Mediterranean produce. There was also *Steak Tartare*, or *Salade Niçoise*, or the ever-popular steak and chips with salad and *green* mustard. And I loved it when, in one of the restaurants, the waiter, with a pencil taken from behind his ear, wrote down our order on the rustic white paper tablecloth, and then produced the bill from it, tearing off the relevant portion. It seemed so simple and chic and fun. Then we would walk in the twilight back to the hotel, before separating and going to bed. It was easy and very enjoyable, and the perfect antidote to the trials of the last two years.

I felt that we became friends and companions during those days; the miserable, former days, when her menopause and our adolescent excesses had caused such conflict, finally forgotten. With her customary wisdom and reserve, my mother didn't press me on the recent events of my life but, in the course of our conversation, it became clear that she knew something was wrong. I was reluctant to approach the matter of my marriage, but somehow the conversation turned in that direction and, over the days that we had together, I began to talk about the events which had so wounded me. It was a slow and hesitant process on my part, not knowing how she would react, and knowing that she believed marriage to be a lifelong commitment; but there was no reproach or criticism of any kind in her response.

She listened to me patiently and quietly, letting the memories trapped in my sad inner chamber come to the fore. And once so exposed and examined, they could be dealt with. She was desperately sorry that my life had taken such a turn, and that I had had to suffer so much; but she assured me of her love and her prayers, and said she would support whatever course of action I felt appropriate. As a result of our conversations, the venom was taken from the sting of the scorpion: recent events, now aired and shared, and seen in their proper light, had no power over me. The scorpion may seek to sting me, I thought, but its tail was now harmless: I could face both the past and the future with equanimity.

Chapter 5 : New Beginnings

I returned from my holiday with a fresh resolve. I would seize the day, grasping life with both hands and, putting the past behind me, make the most of every opportunity. I didn't need to hide any more, or to feel guilty. My friends and family knew of my situation and didn't judge me. Indeed, there was a new attitude in society, which was more accepting and inclusive, in all sorts of areas. I would tough it out if I needed to but, on the whole, thought that that wouldn't be necessary. And so it proved to be. Women were finding that new opportunities were opening up for them in many areas, and qualifications and experience were prized more highly than one's personal life or gender.

But this time, I thought, I will stay firmly in the saddle; I won't let any stranger come into my home and destroy the things that I hold most dear. I will hold the reins so tightly that I will keep my life on its prescribed track and cast aside, by whatever means, the detractors. I can see, with the benefit of hindsight, that that course of action caused me, imperceptibly, to reinforce the protective layer I had already developed around my heart and my emotions, to protect them. I was like an endangered hedgehog: as soon as I perceived a threat from any quarter I would, metaphorically, roll up into a ball and erect a defensive shield of behavioural spines. But in reality I had little to fear: most of my friends and colleagues were not Christians, and I was largely saved from moral judgements.

Did I think at all about God during those years? Mostly not, or if I did it was in the same way as one thinks about the dentist: that I must at some point go for a check-up, and be told off for not flossing, but not yet, not now. I was in my late twenties by this time, and married to the colleague from work who had so kindly befriended me during my earlier crisis. Together we had bought a two-bedroomed flat in Wallington, and in 1975, when I was thirty, our daughter was born. I had had to give up my job as there was no statutory Maternity Leave at that time, but I was happy and fulfilled in my new role as wife and mother. I think the first time I really began to think seriously about God again was when our daughter was born.

It had taken a while to conceive her, and then the birth had been difficult, both for her and for me. I recall looking at her, as she lay beside me on the hospital bed, and wondering – as I'm sure most mothers do – just who had made her, who had designed those clear blue eyes, that pale skin and dark curly hair, the fingers and toes. I had clearly nurtured her and brought her to birth, but I could not say that I had 'made' her. And it was then that the idea of a loving and creative God began to infiltrate my thinking. I did make a tentative approach to my local church to have her christened, by way of thanksgiving for her birth; but so many conditions were placed on it, insisting that we attend church for a certain number of weeks, and submit to a course of instruction, that I abandoned the idea.

Our flat, as I said, was big enough for all of us, but it was on the second floor, without a lift (not easy with a baby, the pushchair and the shopping), and we didn't have our own garden. These factors influenced us sufficiently to convince us of the need to move to a house. We therefore visited many properties which were for sale and, among all the houses we saw, one stands out in my memory. It was an older house, probably built between the two World Wars and decorated in an old-fashioned style, but it had a wonderful 'atmosphere', which I felt it as soon as we crossed the threshold.

It was owned by two elderly sisters, who greeted us warmly, and thoughtfully pointed out the faults of the house, as well as its many benefits. It could have been the right one for us, and I was attracted to it, though it would have needed extensive modernisation.

But of almost greater interest to me was the 'character', of the older of the two sisters, the one who figured most prominently in our visit. She sat on a sofa and invited me to join her, as I was holding the baby and she was getting heavy.

And as I sat near our hostess, I became aware of the wonderful 'atmosphere' that I felt surrounded her. It seemed to be both strong and gentle at the same time, full of love and understanding and acceptance. And it was accompanied by what I can only describe as an 'aroma': not a smell, or a perfume as such, but something sweet but not cloying, and somehow 'clean' and 'light', that played on my senses. I'm sure she was quite unaware of the impression she was making on me, for she responded to us with complete ease and naturalness.

But as I sat next to her and experienced these extraordinary phenomena, I knew that I wanted what she had. I wanted to burrow my face in it. I wanted to grasp hold of it with both hands, and to 'possess' it. Instead I just sat as close as I could, drinking it in and almost gulping it down. Within a year or so I would understand that these were most probably the nine manifestations, or 'fruit' of the Holy Spirit, and listed by the Apostle Paul in his letter to the Christians at Galatia, (Chapter 5:22-23) as: love, joy, peace, patience, kindness, goodness, faithfulness, gentleness and self-control. At that time I didn't know what had generated them, nor how one could obtain them for oneself. And later I was to understand more about the 'smell' I had detected, for it is again the great Apostle Paul who brings clarification when he says: 'But thanks be to God, who always leads us in triumphal procession in Christ, *and through us spreads everywhere the fragrance of the knowledge of him.'* (2 Corinthians 2:14). It was the 'aroma' of Christ that I had detected. And as I sat there I noticed that on the wall was a plaque which said, in old-fashioned writing,

Make Every Issue the Subject of Prayer.

And as I looked at it, it seemed to demand my attention, as though it was flashing at me, like a neon sign. It reminded me of my mother and her Prayer Cell, and of the God whom I had abandoned all those years earlier. In the event we didn't buy that house, but I have never forgotten our visit, or that wonderful older lady, and the simple plaque on the wall. In retrospect I can see that these were divine markers, like tasty crumbs, strewn along the path, which God knew that I would 'eat' and, in so doing, move ever-nearer to Him. What I discovered later was that my mother had prayed for me every day, morning and evening, for most of my life; and I'm sure it was those prayers which had moved His hand to reach down and help me.

Another such incident occurred a couple of years later, after we had finally moved to our chosen house, off the Mortlake Road, in Kew Gardens. I was talking to an older Jewish friend on the subject of marriage and he said how important it was that the couple, husband and wife, did not become so close that they excluded God. I tried to make sure that my face retained its habitual composure as he spoke, but inwardly I was deeply shocked.

Up until that point I had considered God rather as an affable uncle, or an autocratic ruler, or even as a source of life and a maker of babies; but it had never occurred to me that He could be vulnerable, capable of being hurt by our selfish behaviour.

That He might actually live with us, and share His life with us. I had in my mind the picture of three people sitting around a table: two were talking animatedly to each other and the third was entirely excluded. This was a shocking and radical view and one that I still wonder about; but I believe it to be true. That God has chosen to make Himself vulnerable to our love. This was another of the crumbs in my path which were leading me, slowly and gently, ever-closer to their divine source.

The house in Kew Gardens was lovely, with its original windows and doors; and with fireplaces in the bedrooms as well as the reception rooms, some of which also had decorative over-mantels. It had mature gardens to the front and back, the rear garden, with its exotic planting, being over 120 feet long, with red-brick paths. Many houses in that area had unusual and rare plants because of their proximity to the famous botanical gardens. We had a large fig tree which was very prolific, producing two good crops a year. Many of the figs fell to the ground and rotted, simply because we were unable to harvest them all. I very much enjoyed being a mother, but my husband was away from home for many hours each day and I missed the adult company that I had enjoyed when I had worked in the commercial sector. I knew few people locally, and I felt lonely and isolated.

I was very pleased, therefore, when my in-laws moved into the area and, with their support, I was able to take on a very easy and enjoyable job as a sales assistant in a shop in Richmond which sold 'period', (now known as 'vintage') clothing. I was in sartorial heaven! I worked on Wednesday afternoons and Saturdays, initially just handling the sales but, within a few months I was accompanying the owners on buying trips, on Friday mornings, to the dealers' market in Portobello Road. I must have inherited the love of quality clothing from my father, for I could tell by the cloth and the 'cut' what was good. There were stalls selling frocks and blouses, skirts and jackets, ballgowns and wedding dresses, as well as hats, jewellery and every kind of accessory. I observed closely, but stayed silent, as my employers made their own decisions about stock levels, profit margins and general purchasing policies.

But when, a few months later, I was able to secure the lease of a shop of my own in Kingston-upon-Thames, I gave my instinct full rein. I bought not only women's clothing, but also men's: wonderful three-piece suits made from the finest fabrics, constructed carefully with pleats and different sized pockets, so similar to the clothes my father had worn. There were heavy tweed overcoats still bearing their tailor's label; dinner suits and Norfolk jackets, collarless shirts and Fair-isle pullovers, heavy brogues and soft hats. I was only limited by the amount of cash I had on me (never cheques, and don't ask for a receipt!), and the amount I could carry, in black sacks, back to the tube station.

For, laden with cash secreted discreetly about my person, I would take the first train from Kew Gardens, getting out at Hammersmith and walking the short distance to the lovely old Metropolitan Line, then take The Tube to Ladbroke Grove. From there I would walk to Notting Hill Gate and the Portobello Road. In winter it was often bitterly cold and, however much I tried to wrap myself in layers of warm clothing, I would soon get so cold that my numb fingers could barely handle the cash, let alone carry the sacks. Then I would fall into one of the small, fug-laden coffee shops which were dotted around the market, and have a hot drink and a bun. For a time my fingers would ache badly as they thawed out and then suddenly I was strong again, blood coursing freely through my veins, and my mind clear for any final purchases. I became known as a 'regular', and was greeted warmly by the stall-holders, who became my new, if rather unconventional, colleagues.

I also frequented auction houses and, if the price was right, I would buy a 'lot' which might contain a miscellany of items, only a few of which I would use as stock. The rest I would either keep for personal use, or pass on. My mother had clearly been anxious for me as I opened my shop, wondering if I had enough experience to secure its success. I took a more relaxed view, believing it to be the right thing at that time, and thankfully I did succeed. It became a popular venue for all kinds of customer and I worked hard to ensure its success. Only many years later did we understand that many of my German forbears had earned their livelihoods by trading up and down the Rhine; and that one of them, Jakob, had been a tailor in Landau.

Yes, they were happy, stimulating days, and I like to think that I became a better mother as a result of my trading activities. I loved wearing the clothes myself, exulting in the creation of a new style simply by combining various items in an unconventional way. I was tall and slender at the time and could wear men's suits, pinstripe or plain, with or without waistcoat or turn-ups. These I combined with a printed rayon blouse from the thirties or forties, a silk lace handkerchief arranged just-so in the top pocket, and a statement brooch on the lapel. That was my androgynous style. I could also feel deeply feminine in a black cocktail dress from the late nineteen-thirties, or in a simple ditsy-printed rayon dress from the nineteen-forties.

I also enjoyed, and felt strangely empowered by, the sparse and angular garments imposed on society during the War and controlled in every detail – number of buttons, length of sleeve, amount of fabric used - by the War-time government under its 'Utility' label. The injunction to 'Make Do and Mend' certainly resulted in the creation of some very skilfully constructed garments. Occasionally, on a warm summer's day, I would take our daughter with me to the Market, hanging my sacks from the handles of her buggy. She thoroughly enjoyed all the bustle and then simply fell asleep when the mood took her.

But how was I faring as a person, and as a wife? Sadly, I must say, not so well. The relationship with my husband had prospered in adversity, but it now struggled to withstand the conflicting demands of two very different lifestyles. For I had developed a way of life which involved interaction with the slightly 'edgy' world of vintage style and fashion. I had become an agent for a jewellery designer, exhibiting and selling her creations in some famous Knightsbridge stores, as well as hiring out stock to a television company for 'period' dramas; and I worked hard to build up my business. My husband was centred on his work and his sport. It was inevitable, therefore, that we developed different friendships and gradually began to drift apart.

Attempts were made on both sides at reconciliation, but it was clear – to us at least – that the life had gone out of our relationship. We both sought comfort and support in different circles, and in the end, apart from the love we both felt for our daughter, we had practically nothing in common. It was a terrible time, and I felt desperate. I couldn't bear the thought of another marital failure, another divorce. I became depressed and anxious and was prescribed Valium by my doctor. To numb the pain I began to drink whisky, for my husband was given many bottles of spirits at Christmas by grateful clients, and they stood invitingly in the sideboard. I never did, and still don't, like alcohol, and for me whisky is a horrible drink; nevertheless I drank it, in the hope that it would help me to cope with the overwhelming misery that I was feeling.

Many times, even in the morning, I would have a drink, and then brush my teeth, so that the other mothers at the nursery could not detect the fumes on my breath. And then one day, when the combined effects of Valium and whisky made precious little difference to my mood, I took a lip-pencil from my handbag and, on a scrap of paper (it was all I had to hand when the impulse took me), wrote a short letter to God. I just asked Him why my life was in such a mess; was He testing me; and would He help me to get out of it? I kept that letter for years, until the writing was too blurred to read and the paper began to disintegrate. But that letter was momentous, for it marked the end of my rebellion and the point of my surrender to God. From then on things began to change. I was thirty-four and the year was 1979.

Act 3

1979-1995

Chapter 6 : I Surrender

The first thing to happen in response to my 'letter', was the mild curiosity I felt about the location of my Bible. It had been presented to me as a child, as a prize for regular attendance at Sunday School, and the dedication on the frontispiece explained that, and gave my name and date of birth. It was an illustrated Bible, which was hard-backed and covered simply in blue fabric. I thought it might be in the attic; I certainly couldn't see it on the bookshelves. After some considerable time rummaging I found it there, in a pile of old books, all covered in dust and cobwebs. I dusted it off and brought it downstairs, where I sat and held it lightly in my hands. Then I opened it and read the inscription, which had been signed by the vicar, and by the elderly couple who had so faithfully run the Sunday School. Yes, I could remember them, and the Old and New Testaments.

Before I left school I had completed a year of 'A' Level in Religious Studies, and recalled how sad, confused and disillusioned I had become by the popular theories of authorship. That 'Moses' hadn't apparently written the first five books of the Old Testament: that 'Isaiah' was at least two people, if he had ever existed at all; and that 'Matthew', 'Mark', 'Luke' and 'John' were not the authors of their eponymous gospels, rather these were the work of shadowy conspirators called 'L', 'M', 'P', and 'Q'. I held the Bible carefully, because the fabric supporting the spine was disintegrating, and experienced very mixed emotions. Would its contents help and comfort me, or would they bring greater stress and confusion? I had to find out.

Gradually my attention was drawn to the Gospel of John, which in the past had been my favourite Gospel, and read again the 'High Priestly' prayers (found in chapters 13 to 17) offered up by Jesus, shortly before he was killed. And as I read them tears started falling. Not 'sobbing', 'hot' or 'crying' tears, in the accepted form; but much more old-fashioned weeping, as tears just gently but regularly fell, both onto my lap and onto the pages of the Bible itself. This was the beginning of what I subsequently called my 'Vale of Tears', when I would weep for easily an hour, remembering and confessing past sins of commission and omission, and asking God to forgive me. What was extraordinary to me was that this activity didn't leave me with a puffy face and red eyes, as 'normal' crying would have done. On the contrary, when I had to stop and go out, to meet my daughter from nursery school or some other such activity, all I had to do was dry my face and go; there was no indication at all of the time of confession and repentance that I was experiencing in-between times.

This period of confession and weeping lasted for a few weeks and was followed by a time when I felt I needed to forgive certain people. Once I had opened myself up to this new area of activity, it seemed as though the Spirit was impressing on me the fact that I harboured bitterness, anger and resentment towards all sorts of people. Some related to my childhood, some to my family, some to my work colleagues, some towards God Himself. It was shocking to realise what a catalogue of sins committed against me, real or imaginary, I was harbouring.

And so I 'forgave' people and I found that, with each act of forgiveness, I opened my hands: and it was as though that person was then 'released' to leave me; as though my unforgiving-ness had bound them to me, and now both they and I could be free.

It was wonderful, once I had got used to it, as though great shackles which had bound me to my past were broken open, and I could run towards the future. I still rejoice in the fact that we can, in Christ, forgive those whom we perceive to have wronged us. By such forgiveness we can be clear channels of God's love and power; we can start each day with a clean sheet, not harbouring past offences but rejoicing with a clear conscience in our relationship with God and with each other.

But though I was experiencing great joy in my new-found faith, I was by no means fully aware what it all meant, or how it all 'worked'. What weighed most heavily on me was the realisation that I had wanted to do 'the right'; that my intentions were genuinely good, but that somehow, things had become twisted and distorted and had turned out badly, sometimes very badly. And I couldn't understand why. It was only some time later, as I read the Apostle Paul's explanation of the gospel to the believers in Rome saying, 'We know that the law is spiritual; but I am unspiritual, sold as a slave to sin. *I do not understand what I do. For what I want to do I do not do, but what I hate I do.'* (Romans 7:14-15), that I had a measure of understanding. For he seemed to sum up my own situation exactly. I had wanted to live a happy, peaceful and, indeed, respectable, life, and it had all turned to dust in my hands. Where and why had it all gone wrong? And, more importantly, was there any way out? Was I doomed forever to endure this crushing cycle of high hopes and deepest despair? I was desperate for understanding, and didn't know which way to turn.

And then, one Sunday, I suggested to my daughter that we go to church. She had no idea what I meant, but she willingly accompanied me, and we walked the few hundred yards to where it was located, at the end of our avenue and on a junction with two other roads, on a corner. From the outside, with its redbrick façade, it looked conventional enough as a suburban Anglican church. But once inside all preconceptions were instantly swept aside. The interior was much older than the exterior, and brought to mind an old tithe barn. And this is precisely what it was: an old Sussex tithe barn, which had been dismantled and re-assembled, lovingly, carefully, brick by brick and timber by timber, in this leafy corner of south-west London. I instantly loved it, and was content to sit, very unobtrusively, at the back, letting the wonderful atmosphere enter into my soul.

My daughter was soon invited to join the other children in their activities, and I settled myself into the service. Following the pattern of my childhood, I stood for the hymns, and knelt for the prayers and sat for the sermon and the Bible readings. As I heard the Old and New Testament Lessons it was like meeting dear friends, whom I hadn't seen for seventeen years but, although I had changed, they had not. I felt that, after all my prodigal wanderings, I had finally come home, and that God, as my spiritual Father, had run out to meet me. I was possessed of a deep peace and joy, even though my personal circumstances had become desperately bad. My husband had met someone whom he loved and wanted to be with. (He was right; they are still together after nearly forty years, and happy.) Therefore, it seemed, our divorce was inevitable. And this time there was so much more that had to be taken into consideration. What would happen to our daughter, or our house, or my business?

These matters weighed on me, night and day, for months. I believed, and a top firm of London solicitors confirmed this, that I would be granted the 'care and control' of our daughter, but my husband wanted her to live with him and his new family, which also contained young children. I was adamant that this was non-negotiable. I decided to hand over the shop to my business partner, believing that she had the skills and experience to take it forward. As indeed she did. But I wanted to stay in our lovely home and I wanted my daughter with me. But I simply could not work out how to pay for it all, for it was an expensive house in a desirable area. I could not raise the money needed to buy my husband out: my business had been successful, but I hadn't made a lot of money. I pushed so many doors and considered so many options, but each one, in turn, closed on me. I was going round in circles, like a donkey who goes round and round in a confined space, activating a wheel which, in turn, threshes the corn; or a hamster in one of those exercise wheels, expending a great deal of energy but actually going nowhere.

By this time I was a regular attender at church, and had become familiar again with the great stories of the Old Testament. I joined a Bible-study group which met locally, in the home of a dear older woman, and learnt more about the Christian faith, as well as making new friends. I had no idea of this but apparently, in the years since I had been a regular church-goer, certain changes had taken place in some parts of some denominations. This change was called 'The Charismatic Renewal', and celebrated the fact that the Holy Spirit, (who, in my childhood, had been called 'The Holy Ghost'), was active in the Church today, imparting spiritual gifts. This Spirit enabled people to have words of wisdom or knowledge and to understand the spiritual landscape, in a process generally called 'discernment'. It also enabled people to pray 'in the Spirit', (otherwise known as 'tongues', or glossolalia), and to perform miracles - of healing and in other ways - and in this way built up, or 'edified' the Church and equipped believers for every kind of practical and spiritual work.

I was fascinated but suspicious. I have always hated any kind of excess or emotionalism, and have always sought to follow a line which was measured, controlled and predictable. The Church, as I had known it, was just like this, with its round of liturgies and festivals; I wasn't sure that I wanted to have an active part in this new dispensation, with its strong dependence on, and empowerment by, the Holy Spirit. But I didn't dismiss it out of hand, and my lovely home group leader lent me two books which helped me in my search for clarification. One was a slender classic by the great Chinese apologist, Watchman Nee, entitled, *The Normal Christian Life*; the other was *When the Spirit Comes*, by an Anglican priest called Colin

Urquhart. In their different ways they helped me a great deal, bringing a balanced biblical understanding of this new phenomenon.

It was at this time that I made an important new acquaintance, and it came about in this way. I had become friendly with other members of the Bible-study group, and we tended to sit together when we were in church. Accordingly, one Sunday, I sat with a particular friend and, on the other side of her was a young man, tall and with dark hair and a very pleasant face, whom I hadn't seen before. Then he stood up to sing, and as he did so my heart stopped. I had never heard a 'real' singer in the flesh before, and there he was, two seats away from me. He had the most wonderful bass voice, with a richness and modulation that was simply spine-tingling. I took a discreet closer look and assumed that he was the husband of my friend and neighbour. 'No wonder she was always so happy', I thought, rather resentfully. But for some reason she leant towards me during the service and said that he wasn't her husband. How strange. Had she somehow read my thoughts? Why did she tell me that?

It was interesting, I thought, but I had resolved to have nothing more to do with men, and decided to expunge any further curiosity from my mind. I had much weightier things to consider. For not only were there the pressing concerns of the divorce and the settlement; I was also deeply concerned about my spiritual standing, before God. Could I be accepted back into the Church? Would I be allowed to take Holy Communion? Could I be saved from 'hell and damnation', considering my background and all the bad things I knew I had done in my life? These and other related issues were at the forefront of my mind, and I didn't know where to turn for clarification. But clarification did come, and from an unexpected source.

It was the custom at this church to have refreshments at the back of church after the service. For some weeks I had decided not to stay, feeling that I couldn't cope with the uncertainty of it all; that questions might be asked of me that I couldn't, or didn't want, to answer. But on this particular Sunday, sometime in June 1979, I felt that I should stay and trust God for the outcome. In due course the young man with the beautiful voice came and stood beside me and, introducing himself, asked if I lived locally.

I'm sure he was expecting the usual small-talk associated with such situations, but I was in no mood for empty pleasantries. 'Please tell me', I said, having very briefly introduced myself, 'I have been divorced and need to know if I can be saved.' If he was shocked at such a direct question he didn't show it, but looked at me for a moment and then made his reply. 'Yes, 'he said, 'if you are truly sorry for your sins and have repented of them, and if you believe that Jesus died in your place, to take the punishment for all human sin, then, yes, you can be saved.' This was good news indeed, even though I didn't understand at all the concept of Jesus dying to save me from the consequences of my sins. But I could honestly acquiesce with the things he said about confession and repentance, remembering with sharp clarity the recent days I had spent weeping and confessing my sins.

But I had to be sure. 'Are you sure?', I pressed him, because I didn't want 'comfortable' words if, in reality, they lacked any real force or were untrue. Better to know now and face the distressing facts, I thought, than to live in a delusion. But he repeated his reply, giving a little more clarification. That Jesus had died on the cross to take away the sins of the world. That He had died in my place and, instead of condemning me for my sinfulness, He would give to me, as a free gift, His righteousness. It was the first time I had heard of the 'substitutionary sacrifice' explanation of the crucifixion, and although I was ignorant of the Christian faith in so many ways, this made sense to me, wonderful, terrible, sense.

I listened to him and, as I did so, it was as though a messenger of God was speaking to me, calming me and reassuring me of God's love and compassion. I made the short walk home with a lightness of heart that I hadn't felt for years.

Only much later did I learn that this man should not have been at church in Kew at all at this time. He should have been in France, on a language course with his wonderful, redoubtable, polyglot grandmother. But she, some days earlier, had had a fall outside a shop in London and broken her arm, rendering her unable to travel. When I heard of this I detected the divine hand at work: I believed that God had wanted me to hear that message and He knew that her grandson would faithfully deliver it. I think it was the most important meeting and the most profound conversation of my life, and I am eternally grateful for it.

Swiftly the weeks passed and with them I became more at ease in my attendance at church. But there was still one big question that hung over me: was I eligible to take Holy Communion?

I very much wanted to be, with a deep desire to 'feed on', (and God knows how much I needed it), the body and blood of Christ. But I didn't want to take it 'unworthily', as the Christians in Corinth had been in danger of doing, and thereby bring down judgement on myself, (I Cor. 11:27-29). Yet I didn't want to 'ask', and so draw attention to myself. I was already in some turmoil as I sat in the pew, alone, next to the central aisle. As the service proceeded my anxiety grew; and when the time came for members of the congregation to get up from their pews and go forward to the altar- rail, I was in an agony of indecision. I knelt with my head in my hands and my eyes tightly shut, with my heart beating powerfully in my chest, hoping that something would happen to help me.

Suddenly I felt a hand on my shoulder and, believing it to be the church-warden, prompting me that it was my 'turn', I got up and joined the queue. As I did so I turned to give the smallest acknowledgement to the church-warden, but there was nobody there to acknowledge. The church-warden was some distance away, and there was no-one else near me who could have touched me and then moved away in that short space of time. It was shocking but also strangely exhilarating. I felt that God not only knew my thoughts and understood my dilemma; He also provided the direct help I needed to do what I had so wanted to do, not in brazenness or ignorance, but with a clear conscience, in response to the divine prompt.

In the course of the following weeks the young man, (his name was Ian), called on me at home, for he lived nearby, and discussed the faith with me, lending me books and drawing from me, in a sensitive and helpful manner, the circumstances of my life. I hadn't wanted to tell him and thereby disillusion him, but apparently I didn't, for he assured me that sin was sin, whether in small and private ways or, like mine, in 'big' and public ways. And that we all needed to repent, and be forgiven, and avail ourselves of the enormous benefits of the cross. I didn't need persuading. I had been desperate and even at that time, with my growing understanding of the faith, I was like an impoverished beggar, accepting a great basket of food. I received it unreservedly, and with immense gratitude.

However, there were two areas, in particular, in which I wanted clarification. The first was the issue of 'acceptance'; had I really been accepted in the Church, as I had hoped, especially by those who knew of my background? In response, Ian told me more of the 'exchange' that took place when Jesus died on the cross. That in place of my feelings of 'rejection' (whether real or imaginary), I had been given the unconditional 'acceptance' of Jesus. That it did not depend on the opinion or attitude of an individual. It was done completely and immutably by divine grace; and that if people did ever view me with suspicion, or marginalise me, or actually reject me, then I could 'stand' with absolute peace and confidence on the perfect work of the cross.

The second matter concerned the complex subject of righteousness. In all my tears of repentance, the sin that had upset me most was that of my self-righteousness; that I had sought to live in my own righteousness, justifying my own actions and blaming others if things had gone wrong. I could see now that I had offended

God by such an attitude; indeed now, with my new understanding, it seemed to be the most offensive of all my selfish ways. But help was at hand, for Ian explained to me that, instead of the rags and tatters of my own righteousness, I could receive the perfect righteousness of Jesus.

That this was another of the extraordinary exchanges which had taken place through the cross of crucifixion. That I no longer had to justify myself to any friends or strangers who might baulk at, or even recoil from, the circumstances of my life. Instead I could be open and honest, knowing I was free of condemnation and 'covered over' with a divine righteousness which I could never have achieved by my own efforts. Over the years I have learnt a great deal more about the 'exchange' of the cross, but these two explanations were sufficient for those times and circumstances, and they have remained with me, as eternal truths, in all the intervening years.

For two other events occurred in my life at this time, both momentous and life-changing, but touching upon very different matters. The first involved the practice which I knew some Christians exercised, of 'speaking in tongues', or 'praying in the Spirit'. I knew that it was often referred to in the New Testament, with the Apostle Paul saying he prayed in tongues more than anyone, (I Corinthians 14:18). I was sceptical. Was it just a gift which was available to the early Church, or was it still in operation today? Would it disrupt, or even divide congregations if some members exercised the gift, and others couldn't, or wouldn't? And how would one know if it was a genuine work of the Spirit, rather than the excesses of an overactive imagination? All these questions assailed me, but I felt that I could not evade the issue. And so I read as much as I could, and prayed for clarification, and then one day, when I was at home alone, I thought I would 'have a go'. I sat on the sofa in the living room and composed myself, confessing and repenting of my sins, for I knew that the Spirit would not work through a channel which harboured sin. I then laid hands on myself.

It wasn't the first time that hands had been laid on me. I had been 'confirmed' in our local Anglican church at the age of twelve, and had anticipated with bated breath the moment when I would kneel before the presiding bishop and wait for him to lay his hands on me. I didn't know what to expect, but I did believe that, whatever 'it' was, it would be real and dramatic. But nothing happened, not even a light tingling, and nothing like the inner thunder I had hoped for. And so I returned sadly to my pew, believing that, for me at least, it hadn't 'worked'. Therefore my expectations were not high when, some twenty years later, I laid hands on myself. I sat there, quite still, wondering if the Spirit would graciously bestow this gift, but again nothing happened. I sat for longer and still nothing happened, and I was just about to give up, when I felt the prompt that I should be more pro-active. That I should take a deep breath, and move my lips and exercise my vocal chords, as though I was about to speak. And so, and with a measure of desperation, this is what I did. And suddenly words began to flow, but they were not words that I knew, though it did have the slightly 'sighing' cadence of Hebrew, which I had heard quite often.

I was so happy at this turn of events, euphoric really; but I was also awestruck and a little fearful. For I knew that it was the Spirit Himself who was working in me and through me, in some divine partnership; He of perfect wisdom, love, power and understanding, and little sin-prone me. But that was the truth of it. I continued to pray in this way for some time - I've no idea how long - and suddenly it seemed to me as though the room became brighter, as though someone had switched on a light. Very tentatively I opened my eyes, but could see nothing untoward. Nonetheless, I had the feeling that I wasn't alone. As I prayed I breathed deeply, and could feel some kind of power entering my body, not quite like electricity, more like the flowing of a river.

I knew from my reading of the New Testament that one edifies oneself when praying in the Spirit, as well as interceding for all the saints (that is, the believers), according to the will of

God (Romans 8:27). Gradually the light returned to its normal level and I stopped 'speaking'.

I have continued to exercise this gift ever since, and almost always when I'm alone, or else very discreetly. Only once have I felt the prompt to 'give a tongue' in a public meeting, and when it came, my heart was in my mouth. But I did it, nonetheless. It flowed easily and lasted less than a minute, and I was so relieved when someone present, a respected member of that congregation, fluently and clearly, gave the interpretation (see 1 Corinthians 14:27-28). I consider this gift as one of the most precious, and yet most flexible, of all the gifts bestowed by the Spirit: for it can be exercised both privately and publicly, it can provide a powerful outlet in good times and bad; and it enables us to pray according to the will of God, even when we don't know what that will is. I try to pray in this way each day; sometimes for only five minutes, sometimes for longer, for it also 'edifies' me, and I often feel that I am in desperate need of that. And, under wise moderation, there is no need for it to divide congregations. On the contrary, it should strengthen, build up, and unite them.

The second event related to the domestic front, where there had been new developments. For I had bowed to the inevitable and agreed to the sale of the house. I had heard somewhere - from the radio, I think – that properties in East Anglia were half the cost of a house in London, and I thought that we, my daughter and I, could move there and live simply, within our means. I had never been to East Anglia, and wasn't really sure what such a move would entail, but at least it provided me with a way forward.

Accordingly our house was put on the market; and then, one Sunday around this time, my husband took us out for lunch to an up-market burger restaurant in Sheen. It was a lovely meal, and we seemed to relate easily to each other, although nothing had changed in terms of our proposed divorce. In hindsight, I think the change had come about because the Spirit had been doing a work of grace in my life, enabling me to be kinder and less critical or unkind.

One saying of Jesus in particular, recorded in the Gospel of John, had been having a profound influence on me. It is that recorded in chapter 12 verse 47, and says simply, 'For I did not come to judge the world, but to save it.'. That fundamentally changed my perception of life and my motivation in living: I suddenly wanted to align myself with Jesus' purposes, and that influenced everything I was doing. Certainly the change in my reactions was not the result of my own will, but I was conscious that I was more gentle and responsive than I had been for years, if ever. Therefore, when the surprise question came from my husband, when we were on the dessert course, I didn't dismiss it out-of-hand, shocking though it was. For he asked again if he could have custody our daughter; not because, as he said, he had a right to her, but because it lay within my gift to 'give' her.

I was stunned for a moment and looked across to her as she was about to attack an ice-cream of wondrous size and construction. She was wearing a very chic French outfit: a straw hat, with a simple floral dress, co-ordinating socks and almond-green suede shoes. She was deeply engrossed with her dessert and had no idea of the magnitude of the events which were taking place around her. And as I looked at her it seemed as though Time itself stood still.

As though I was still thinking and moving, but everyone and everything else seemed to have stopped. And in that time the story, baffling and heart-rending as it is, of Abraham and Isaac, came to mind. That God had given Isaac to Abraham as a precious gift in his old age, and then asked Abraham to offer him back. And Abraham obeyed though, thankfully, a substitute sacrifice was found and Isaac's life was saved. It is a shocking story but, in the 'time' that I had, I felt that God was asking the same thing of me. Not 'telling' me, just saying that this was what He was asking, and that she would not suffer because of it: on the contrary, this would be for her best.

Strangely there was never any doubt in my

mind; I knew that this was the divine solution, and I was about to say 'yes', when my husband said that I should think about it overnight and let him know in the morning. I agreed to that, and then thought of nothing else for the rest of the day, long after he had dropped us off. The responsibility I felt was almost overwhelming, as well as the pain in my heart. The next morning I phoned him and told him of my decision. I was still possessed of the peace I had felt the day before, although the consequences of that decision were beginning to dawn on me.

It was as though I was a tent, which had been secured to the ground by three guy ropes: my business, my home and my family. And then, within an incredibly short space of time, each one of those guy ropes had been severed, and I was in real danger, metaphorically speaking, of just floating away. I didn't know now, or even care, where I was going to live: it could be in East Anglia, but it could equally be in Timbuctoo or on the other side of the moon. I prayed that God would hold me tightly during this time, as I came to terms with the depth and complexity of my new situation; and asked for very clear guidance about my next move. And that prayer was quickly and clearly answered though, again, from an unexpected source.

For Ian, who had now returned to Cambridge to continue his studies at Trinity College, (where he was both an Open Scholar [Modern Languages] and Choral Exhibitioner), called me within a day or so. Apparently, a note had been pinned to his door by a fellow Modern Linguist. She had a room spare in her student-house, and did he know of anyone who might be suitable? And he, knowing my situation, had thought of me. Was I interested? This was indeed a most unexpected turn of events, but it was at least in East Anglia, I thought.

So I heard myself say that, yes, I would be interested, and he said he would pass the message on. Which he did, and I was summoned to Cambridge to be interviewed by a panel of four, two undergraduate female students and two male post-graduates, as to my suitability. Would I pay the rent on time, as well as my portion of the bills? Yes. Would I take my turn on various rotas, housework, shopping, cooking, washing up? Yes. Would I be prepared to take my turn in visiting an elderly gentleman with multiple sclerosis, who lived at the end of the road, talking with him and preparing him for bed? Yes. Think I would have said 'yes' to anything. I must have passed muster because, shortly after, I was invited to join them.

And so, one Saturday soon after, (it was autumn by now, in 1979), my husband, with our daughter, drove me up to my new home. It was a late-Victorian terraced house, off the Mill Road, and my room was what would probably have been a study, on the ground floor.

It was small, with a bed, some shelves and a wardrobe, with French windows which opened on to the back garden. They helped me to unpack: books on the shelves and clothes in the wardrobe, and saw the bathroom and kitchen which I shared with the other occupants. I had very few possessions, but noticed that there was no waste-paper bin. 'I need a waste-paper bin', I said, like a mantra, repeating it over and over in my head. I was too numb to think coherently of anything. At this point they drove me to Parker's Piece, where they dropped me off and waved goodbye, and I set off for the shops.

I can recall very little from those early days, except that Ian had left a postcard on my bed, welcoming me to Cambridge and hoping that I would be happy there. That helped me a lot; it was a link with the past and gave me strength when I felt very vulnerable. But now I needed a job, if I was going to make good on my assurances to my young interlocutors and pay my way. But what job? My CV made unusual reading, and I assumed that Cambridge would be awash with people, highly-qualified, who wanted to earn some money and enjoy the pleasures of the town. But, through a friend of Ian's, I was told that there was a vacancy at Cambridge University Press, where the Director of Bibles and Religious Books was looking for a Personal Assistant. Would I think it appropriate to apply for that? Yes, I thought it would. I had absolutely nothing to lose.

From this point events moved swiftly. I was interviewed on the following Friday; and on the Saturday a letter was put through my door, telling me that I had been successful, and asking if I could start on the Monday. Indeed, I could, and did. Even now I feel that this was the divine hand at work: I am not a brilliant PA, but I needed a job, not only for money's sake, but also for my own sanity. I couldn't vouch for my conduct if, under those extreme circumstances, I had been left to my own devices in that house for very long. And so, with amazing speed, new and unexpected guy ropes had been attached, and I was secured to the ground, albeit alien ground, by these new developments. As it turned out, I would stay in Cambridge and the University Press for just over three years, and in that time a very great deal happened.

Chapter 7 : The Cambridge Years

Cambridge is a cold place, with an east wind which blows straight across the fens from Siberia. I needed new and warm clothes, a thick coat and stout waterproof boots: my elegant but insubstantial clothes, drawn mostly from my Portobello Road trawls, were simply not practical. Gradually my simple life took shape. I would walk to work, up the Mill Road, across Parker's Piece and then along to Botolph Lane, where – in a converted late-medieval cottage - the Bibles and Religious Books Department was housed. I loved that cottage, where the floors, walls and ceilings all sloped at different angles. I had pleasant and kind colleagues; I was taught how to make the (good, filter) coffee and I took turns with the washing-up. I seemed to pick up the reins of the job quite easily and I enjoyed learning about the specialised world of academic publishing.

At the end of the day I would reverse my journey, reflecting on the day and, when I remembered, praying in the Spirit as I walked. Each day was like a sealed unit. I had no sense of 'continuity'; I just thought 'today I will do this', or 'today I will do that'. There was no sense of progression or connection with the past or with the future. Only the present mattered, or even existed. I had no hope, but strangely I wasn't depressed. Indeed, I had long given up drinking whisky and taking Valium. I just felt numb. I understand that this is a common reaction to shock, grief and loss.

Ian was now busy with his studies, but I saw him quite often, usually in the Chapel at Trinity, where he sang bass in the choir. I was grateful that he introduced me to his fellow students with respect and warmth: I felt that my past, both personal and professional, might have separated me from this privileged and academic fraternity (Trinity was still all-male at this time), by an unbridgeable gap. But that was not the case. Sometimes, on a Sunday, when I wasn't in London visiting my daughter, we would drive into the countryside and admire Gog and Magog, the two small outcrops which is all that Cambridge can call 'hills'. Or sometimes we went to the tea-room in Grantchester. I was learning to love Cambridge, with its bookshops and coffee-houses, its beautiful old colleges and its lively, stimulating people. Sometimes I would go to a concert in Great St Mary's, the big old University Church, and it is from there that a new aspect was unexpectedly brought to my Christian journey, and it came about in this way.

One of my colleagues at work was a secretary, who sat next to me, and we enjoyed each other's company. She was about mid-term pregnant with her first baby, when some abnormality was believed to have been detected. Understandably she was deeply concerned, and shared those concerns with me. What could I do, apart from comfort her and say that I was sure everything would be all right? But I so wanted to do more. And so, one lunch-hour, I dropped into Great St Mary's, which was very near, and began to pray for her. I prayed that God would spare her baby and that it would be born with no abnormality. I stayed there for about a quarter of an hour and, as I left, one of tour guides told me that there was a little chapel just to the left of the altar, which had been set aside for private prayer. I had a little look and was immediately drawn to it. It was simple, and peaceful and private and I wanted nothing more. And so began a pattern of praying in my lunch-hour.

I prayed, of course, for my daughter and her new family, asking that God would bless her and protect her, and give her the grace she needed to cope with her new situation. I prayed for my friends and for my larger family. And I prayed for myself as well, asking God to give me the grace and skills I needed to lead this new and challenging life. I am delighted to say that my friend gave birth to a strong and healthy baby boy, who displayed no abnormalities.

I was so pleased for her, and that stimulated me to further prayer, this time not for someone that I did know, but for thousands whom I did not. For the Falklands War was just beginning and I felt that if anything would influence the conflict for good, it would be prayer. I didn't know it at the time, but this was the beginning of a new, important and exciting development in my Christian walk, which would bear much greater fruit in the years ahead.

In this way the days passed and the following year my divorce became absolute. We had already sold the house in London and, with my portion, I was indeed able to buy a small Victorian terraced house in Cambridge, in the same road in which I was living. It was a former workman's cottage which had been well-modernised: downstairs there was one large living/dining area with a brick fireplace and a pretty open staircase dividing it, and a good-sized kitchen which, in turn, led onto a patio and garden. There were two bedrooms upstairs, and a bathroom, and the front-door opened directly onto the pavement. The relief I felt, when I could finally shut the front door and know that I was in my own home, was immense.

I am grateful for the time in the student-house, but it was often stressful and I rarely felt really relaxed. During my time there one of my fellow-occupants had attempted suicide, and there had often been real tensions, though not directly concerning me. There is one particular event from that time that does deserve a special mention, and centres around a friend of one of my fellow-tenants, who came to stay for a few days.

She was a tomboy-ish person, who drank heavily, swore freely, and was quite rebellious, notwithstanding that her father was a senior churchman. I asked her, following some really unacceptable behaviour, why she conducted herself in this way. She said she was unhappy and depressed, and this is how she dealt with those feelings. I asked her why she didn't pray about things, and she said, why should she, God never answered her prayers. And so I said, what would she pray for, if she did pray; and she said that she would pray that her football team, West Ham, would win the cup. I knew nothing of football or 'the Cup', but I said I would, and did, pray with her that her team would win it.

And I thought no more about it until, the following Spring when, and against all the odds, West Ham did indeed win the FA Cup. I had had no idea at the time that West Ham was at the bottom of the Second Division, and that 'the Cup' was the highly-prized FA Cup. As in all prayer, one can take absolutely no credit for its efficacy: could my prayers really have influenced the outcome of the FA Cup? No-one knows. Answered prayer is a mystery which flows from the throne of God, but I have often thought of this event, and been both amused and encouraged by it.

Work at the Press was, in turns, challenging and interesting; for along with the normal round of book publication and Bible printing, a new book was in preparation, for use in services within the Anglican Communion, called *The Alternative Service Book*.

This was the first revision of the Prayer Book since 1662, and had taken years to bring to fruition, involving a consortium of publishers as well as teams of theologians and translators. All those involved in its publication were sworn to secrecy until the day of its publication, but one publisher jumped the gun and went public the day before its release. That was considered to be very bad form, but publishing, even 'religious' publishing, is a highly-competitive market and some may consider such action entirely justifiable. I understand that the 'ASB', as it is known, is still in use in some parts of the world-wide Anglican Communion.

While working at the Press I met a range of people, the like of whom I hadn't met before; not only the predictably able students and post-graduates, but also some of the more exotic characters who populated that specialised academic environment. One such was an elderly gentleman who knocked one day at the front door of the cottage which housed our office.

I assumed he was some kind of tramp, with his heavily-worn clothes and dishevelled demeanour. He informed me he had something for me and rummaged around in the string-bag he was carrying. Eventually, from among the vegetables it contained, he extracted a parcel. It was a manuscript, produced on A4 paper, and bound together by the sticky strips that surround the great pages of postage stamps which the Post Office produces and sells. I thanked him and he went on his way. It was apparently a long-awaited work of enormous importance, and he was a distinguished academic.

By a strange turn of events, I also met John Robinson at this time. He was Dean of Chapel at Trinity, and it was his custom to invite choir members and their guests to join him for breakfast in his rooms after Chapel on Sunday mornings. I often went, as Ian's guest, and got to know him quite well. He had become a passionate campaigner in the cause of the Palestinians, and he used these breakfast gatherings to attract support for their complex cause. By then he had become far more conservative in his theological views, having published, some five years earlier, a book called, 'Re-dating the New Testament'. This, from biblical textual evidence, made the dates in which it was written considerably earlier than those suggested by previous biblical scholars. I was sad to hear that he had died in 1983; I never said anything about the effect his earlier book had had on me.

Important changes took place within the Press itself while I was there, the most important of which was that, along with many other scattered departments, we moved to new, elegant, purpose-built, open-plan premises on the edge of the town. At the same time I moved from Bibles and Religious Books to be PA to the Editors of Music, Drama and Latin American Studies. Other changes occurred in the operation of the Press itself: the age-old practice of in-house production stopped, with many of the processes now being carried out much more cheaply (if perhaps not always so accurately), in South-East Asia.

Many books were produced by a photographic, rather than a printing process, and paperbacks became more common-place. I am glad that I had been there when the typesetters still did their skilled and speedy work, and when galley-proofs were an essential part of the printing process. It was always a thrilling moment when a typescript finally appeared as a book, having taken months to advance through its various stages of production.

Editing and sub-editing were essential stages of production and just one of the sub-editors remains vividly in my memory. He worked on his own in the cottage next door to ours in Botolph Lane. He had been a Cambridge graduate who, in the course of the Second World War, had had his ear-drums permanently damaged as the result of action as a member of a tank corps. I would often take him coffee in the morning and tea in the afternoon and would always find him in the same state: at his desk with shoes off, smoking a thin black cigar, and reading aloud, painstakingly, each word that he was proof-reading. He couldn't hear himself at all, but he was a dear man and the very best proof-reader.

With the passing of time there came a lessening of the pain of separation from my daughter. We had continued to meet every two weeks and I could see that she was settled and happy in her new family. Mercifully there had been a great deal of goodwill, hard work and commitment extended by all parties to this new arrangement, which had produced a very positive result.

She had changed school and made new friends; and I believe that the 'success' of this whole process of the re-formation of her family was due, in very large part, to her adaptability and, more than that, her courage and fortitude. It wasn't easy for any of us, but she inspired me to keep going. If there were issues which concerned me, I learnt to share them with God in prayer, and found great comfort and reassurance in His gracious response. And then, having lived without it for years, hope unexpectedly returned.

I had become accustomed to life without it, not in a depressed way, but simply not being able to hope for anything. But one Spring morning, as I resumed my attempts to relieve my poorly head. And so we knew that, at some point when circumstances permitted and it was 'right', that we would marry. But I knew little of Ian at that time save that he was highly intelligent and kind and polyglot; that he could act and had a beautiful singing voice.

We thought, as I said, that we would test the waters regarding options for his future career and see what happened. Our enquiries led us first to a famous director of plays who lived in North London and invited us to lunch. He had directed Ian at Cambridge and knew of his abilities.

He was warm in his praise, but seemed reluctant to recommend acting as a career, saying how uncertain and bitchy it all was, and how difficult to get an Equity card, so essential in securing parts. On the whole we felt it was a negative response and decided to close that book and examine instead the possibility of becoming an Anglican priest. To this end Ian booked an appointment with the Diocesan Director of Ordinands in Cambridge and arranged to meet him in his elegant rooms. I came with him and stayed in the car, outside.

The meeting, which lasted well over two hours, was warm and encouraging, with just one important reservation. Best to ditch the young lady he wanted to marry, advised the DDO, because her track record would hold him back. I felt crushed as I heard this, with all the old feelings of rejection rushing back, and had to say that I would, of course, separate myself from the relationship if he felt that any 'call' must have priority. But Ian was adamant. He knew that he wanted us to marry; he wasn't sure about the Anglican ministry. And in this way the decision was made, he would train to be a teacher. Accordingly, he enrolled at Homerton College in Cambridge for a one-year Post-Graduate Certificate in Education, to begin his training in the autumn.

During our time in Cambridge we had largely seen Trinity Chapel as our place of worship, and I recall with great affection the many beautiful choral services I attended there. But we also visited, when we could, a house church in one of the local villages. And it was here that we came into contact for the first time, with the ministry of deliverance. It is one of the less well-known ministries of the Church, and when it is known of, it is often misunderstood. We both became involved in this work, as the need arose, and rejoiced when people, who had clearly been suffering from supernatural oppression, suddenly felt free of it.

It is not always right to 'deliver' people, we found, because they could be rendered more vulnerable as a consequence; but when the circumstances were right, then it was life-changing. We recognised the benefits, indeed the necessity, of working in teams in this ministry, and of being fully submitted to the will of God oneself. But, on the whole, we felt that our knowledge of Christ's ministry on earth grew as a result of those experiences.

Another development on the 'spiritual' front was that I, now secure in my new home, and feeling more positive about the future, could look more critically at the past. In particular I had to examine myself to see if there was any reason why so much pain and disruption had characterised my life so far. And this examination produced an interesting result, for I saw, or I believed that God showed me, that it was my heart that was the cause of this, for it was not only damaged, but broken. And in that state, as a cracked jug is not able to hold water, it had been unable to 'hold' love, or give it or receive it.

In a strange way I felt sorry for myself, not in a self-pitying way, but in a compassionate way, for I believe that it had been broken when I was a small child, when my father died. I had simply been too young to grieve, and the weight of my pain had broken my heart. And so I prayed that God would bind up my broken heart, and that He would gently break down the great walls and ramparts I had built up over the years to protect myself. For I saw that this heart had simply been unable to love properly, and the pain of the years had largely been a consequence of that simple fact. Gradually the great inner chamber which had contained so much grief and pain was emptied. The love I felt for 'God my Father' had overcome the almost unbearable loss I had felt at the death of my own dear father. I don't think one ever fully recovers from the loss of someone one loves; but I do believe that, under God's hand, that loss can be turned into something beautiful for His Kingdom.

In the course of time my prayers for healing were answered; and I gradually found that, like a pump which starts slowly and fitfully, but then becomes stronger and more rhythmic, so my heart was able to both give and receive love. Indeed, I could feel it flowing through me in all sorts of unexpected situations, and I still marvel at the power of God to transform something so damaged into something so strong. It was at this point that I made an important decision: I would adopt God as my father. Jesus said that he had come to reveal the Father (John 17:26); and the great prayer, known as 'The Lord's Prayer', begins with, 'Our Father'.

I realised that I could have a Father who would never leave me: one who could give me the comfort, protection and reassurance I had longed for since losing my natural father all those years ago. And so it is still: I share my deepest thoughts and prayers with Him, and I have developed a real sense, over the years, that

He enjoys such a relationship. And it is not a relationship which is exclusive to me: I believe He is very willing to be 'adopted' by any who call on Him in this way.

By the spring of 1982 Ian's time at Homerton was coming to an end, and we wondered where he would teach. We assumed it would be at one of the neighbouring towns, in the school where he had done his Teaching Practice, and where we knew a suitable vacancy would soon occur. We had been married in March 1981, and it was good finally to live together. My preparation for that event had not been straightforward for, a few days before our wedding (which was a very quiet affair), I suffered from what I believe is known as anaphylactic shock.

I had known for some time that serious tensions had been developing within me about taking this new step. My heart and my mind wanted to move forward and embrace the present and the future wholeheartedly, while my experience and my memories urged against it, reminding me of past wounds and disappointments. I felt that some kind of crisis was looming and, one evening, when I came back from work, the storm broke. Within a shockingly short space of time my throat closed over, as did my eyes, and I could hardly speak or breathe. My face swelled up and turned rather purple, and I just had enough strength to dial 999, before I collapsed into a chair.

I am so grateful that a doctor arrived very soon after and injected me with what I believe was antihistamine. The swelling immediately started to go down. I later discovered that such an attack can be caused by acute anxiety; that was certainly the situation in my case. I wanted to marry Ian and knew him to be a good man who would care for me and never knowingly hurt me; but the knowledge that I might be putting myself at risk of great pain again had caused this extreme reaction. Thankfully the swelling had gone down by the time we were married, a few days later and, thirty-seven years later, I have never regretted that decision.

There have been occasional difficulties and challenges but, overall, it has been better than I could ever have anticipated. At that time we had no expectation, or intention, of leaving Cambridge but, one day, Ian's eye was drawn to an advertisement, for a teacher of languages, in a school in South-West London. He felt it right to apply, (rather than wait for the other post to be advertised), which he did, with my full support. His application was successful and suddenly the path became clear: I would leave the Press, we would sell our little house, and move back to London. The next chapter of our life together had now begun.

known Christian singer and song-writer called Garth Hewitt. This was to celebrate Tearfund's fifteenth anniversary as an organisation: it is extraordinary to know that, this year, they will be celebrating fifty years of service, having started from very small beginnings in 1968.

In due course we sold our house in Cambridge and, not knowing where to move to in London, were thrilled when a colleague at Tearfund, who was also a church warden at a large local church, asked us if we would we be willing to live in a curate's house, in New Malden, which was empty and at risk from being vandalised. Of course not. Delighted! And so our furniture was taken out of store and we moved in, and stayed there for some months, before buying a three-bedroomed terraced house in the area. It was bigger than our house in Cambridge, but perhaps not quite so 'pretty'.

Nonetheless, we were very happy there, and it worked perfectly with our lifestyle, particularly as my daughter was now a frequent visitor and often stayed for a whole weekend.

But, after some two years had passed, Ian was aware that, though his languages (particularly German) were good in theory, he hadn't spent as much time as he would have wanted in Germany to become really fluent, simply because ill-health had curtailed his undergraduate year abroad. He therefore contacted the Central Bureau for Academic Visits and Exchanges and wondered if he could arrange to spend a year in Germany, to 'brush up'.

His school was supportive of such a move, as was Tearfund, and eventually he was accepted, and posted to a pleasant town in north Hessen, south-east of Kassel, called Eschwege. The year was 1985, and Germany was still a divided country, with the border running very close to the area in which we were to live. Although we had visited Germany many times before, we had never heard of this town nor visited this area, and so we studied maps and read up all we could, in preparation. The programme literally worked on two teachers exchanging 'lives' with each other, not only their teaching commitments, but also their homes. Accordingly we prepared our home for its new occupants, making sure that all was clean and functional; but as I worked I was aware that I was excessively tired, and that I had odd pains in my tummy. A simple test revealed what I had suspected, that I was pregnant, and it was in these new and challenging circumstances that we packed up the car and set off for Germany.

Chapter 9 : A German Interlude

It was a long drive to Sontra, the small town a few kilometres from Eschwege, where we were to live, in a small first-floor flat. I was stiff and tired when we finally arrived, and Ian had literally to push me out of the car, before I could compose myself sufficiently to greet the small group of local people who had come to meet us. I wanted just to turn round, and go all the way back home, and climb into My Own Dear Bed, and rest, giving the best support that I could to the young life within me. Instead I heard myself saying, 'Es freut mich!, Es freut mich!' ('I'm pleased to meet you!'), as I had been taught, as I went along the line, shaking hands. These dear people who, in time, became close and lasting friends, helped us with our belongings, and settled us as best they could into our new home. The shock for me was that it was only German that was spoken, and much of that in a local dialect. I hadn't learnt German at school, (indeed I don't think it was even on the curriculum), but both Ian and his grandmother had taught me as much as I could absorb, in the few months that I had before we left.

But nothing had prepared me for this total immersion in the language: only the teachers of English in the school were prepared to speak to me in English. That was a deep concern of mine, but much more pressing by far was the health of the baby I was carrying. For my pains had persisted and I knew I needed medical attention: but I wasn't able to arrange that until I had obtained a referral from some medical practitioner, and I couldn't access that until I had been registered with a medical insurance company. It was a Catch-22 situation and all the time the pains, with my anxiety, were increasing.

Eventually Ian explained our situation to our kindly headmaster, who quickly made the necessary arrangements, and I finally saw a gynaecologist. He rubbed his forehead as he looked at the ultra-sound scan and said, '*Es ist zu klein*!'. I understood that much: the baby was too small. He admitted me to hospital but that night, alone in my hospital room, I lost the baby. It was the worst possible beginning to my time in Germany. I felt that my faith was again in tatters. Why had God raised my hopes of being a mother again (I was forty at this time), only to dash them again? What was the purpose of it? What was the good in it? I could find nothing redemptive in it. For many weeks I was unable to pray, feeling I couldn't ask for anything with any kind of certainty. I felt crushed and abandoned, and all the time this German-speaking world was going on around me, but I couldn't access it, because I couldn't communicate. I became depressed and tearful in the flat when Ian was in school, and I felt that I was falling, deeper and deeper, into the black hole that was opening up around me. It was a desperate time, but help was at hand and, again, it came from an unexpected source.

For Ian had told the Headmaster of our situation, and he, with the teaching colleagues, devised a plan. This was, that I would attend school each day with Ian, not as a teacher, but as a 'pupil', joining in all classes except French and English, and 'learn' with the children themselves. This would give me a routine, and it would help me with my acquisition of German. I was full of trepidation as I began this programme, but it worked, for - from studying Maths with the 10-year olds, to History with the 18-year olds - I was occupied, and challenged, in equal measure. I kept a large notebook, in which I wrote every new word and phrase and, though my head would be spinning at the end of the day, I did make serious inroads into my understanding of German. I made huge mistakes on a daily basis but I pressed on, knowing that the alternative was the empty flat, and the contemplation of how things might have been. Anything was better than that, even embarrassment.

Autumn turned to winter and it was one of the coldest winters on record; temperatures often fell to below -20 degrees Celsius at night, with snow lying on the ground for months, and still falling in April.

We attended the Methodist Church in Eschwege,

and it was our joy to meet the Polish pastor and his wife most Tuesday mornings, for breakfast in their flat. They would provide the butter and the jams, the fruit juice and the wonderful coffee (strong but not bitter); it was our job to provide the rolls. To do this we would leave our flat at just after 6.00 am to drive in the dark to our favourite baker. It was often snowing, and cars would be parked in the slush outside the bakery, as their drivers rushed in to get their fresh, warm rolls. The recollection of those times is still strongly with me: the contrast of the dark and cold outside combined with the warmth and bright lights within, and the calm efficiency of the staff as they served the growing queue of customers. It was then a quick dash to our friends' flat for breakfast before we had a time of prayer.

I still found it hard to pray, but I felt that I was less rebellious towards God. Clearly no answer was to be had about 'why', and so I stopped 'asking'. Instead I sought to 'put on Christ', each day, inviting Him to take the strain of living, so intensively, in a 'foreign' environment, which I was finding almost impossible to bear. And it seemed to work. For I saw myself – as I got out of bed each morning - as one entering some kind of capsule, rather like a diving bell. This enabled me to become part of things; but 'the slings and arrows', which would have entered, and wounded me, in my weakened state, were deflected and bounced off.

village along our journey, to pray and share tea together. Their young children were playing boisterously, but we were able to have a short time alone together, and we prayed 'that', (and I can still recall the words), 'the Wall would disappear', a sentiment and prayer expressed, no doubt, by many Christians during the life of the Wall.

As I prayed, I felt quite small and impotent, having absolutely no idea how such a prayer could, or would, be answered. In the bustle of the ensuing months, I forgot about that occasion, until three years later when, in 1989, I saw on television people with picks and hammers literally destroying the Wall. Incredibly it did just disappear, being broken into various-sized chunks, to be used as souvenirs. Somewhere we have a small piece ourselves, given by a Swiss friend, and covered in garish paint.

The third event, and broadly related to the second, was the low-key activity we did some Sunday afternoons, when the weather was fine, of 'tracking the border'. I have mentioned that we lived near the border with former East Germany, and in our region much of that border was obscured in countryside and woodland. It is a beautiful part of Germany; and in that long cold winter it was often spectacular, as the ground was frequently covered in deep and crunchy snow. And so it was no hardship to us, to drive as far as we could, and then walk the rest of the way, until we came to the red-, black-and gold-striped post, that indicated this was the border. Often the road would just stop, or a railway line run out. Signs in German and English warned the visitor to take care as they were approaching No-Man's-Land. At this point we would stop and pray, with usually only the birds for company, asking for God's blessing and protection on those living in the area.

Sometimes we drove to the villages which were dotted along the border, and saw the great multi-layered fence, as it snaked between the different communities, dividing families. Loudspeakers could be seen in villages in the 'eastern' sector, hanging from trees and lamp-posts, from which messages from Soviet-inspired, East German leaders, regulated the impoverished lives of their inhabitants. I can't recall exactly how we prayed, or whether 'Unification' was on our minds at all, but we were overjoyed when this cruel and ugly border finally came down and families could be reunited. No doubt many Christians were called to do similar things along different parts of the border; we were just a link in a chain. But it was extraordinary, in the ensuing years, to see those same border guards – who had once seemed so threatening, with their razor-sharp fences and watchtowers, their guns and dogs – now, with caps tilted onto the back of their heads, and smoking cigarettes, smiling and posing with tourists for photographs.

In this way we saw the year in Germany through. My German had improved immeasurably, and I am still so grateful for the opportunities that were afforded me, to learn so much, in that warm and accepting environment. I was immensely proud to receive a *Zeugnis* (School Report) from the teaching staff when we left, commending me for my diligence and good attendance. We left in the July of 1986 and Ian returned to his former job, while I wondered what my chances might be of resuming work at Tearfund, as I saw out my pregnancy. They were very understanding of my situation and work was found for me which kept me going until a week before Jonathan was born. A new dispensation was about to begin as I prepared to nurture a young life again, but the year in Germany, with its joys and sorrows, had been a wonderful and unforgettable experience.

Chapter 10 : The London Years (Part Two)

It was good to be back in England, back in our own home and now having a lively baby son to occupy us. I didn't work outside the home for a year after Jonathan was born, and then I only worked part-time, doing clerical and secretarial work. One of the organisations I worked for was 'Christian Friends of Israel' which, as its name suggests, sought to promote good relations between Christians and Jews, particularly those living in Israel, who were often misrepresented and even maligned in the Press. I learned a lot during that time, from entirely reliable sources, about information which rarely reaches the news. We had for some time supported the excellent Anglican organisation called CMJ, or Church's Ministry Among Jewish people, and we found ourselves living in a kind of hybrid world, where we celebrated both the Christian and Jewish festivals, including Passover.

To identify more closely with the world of the Jews I experimented with 'keeping kosher', that is, having essentially two departments in the kitchen, one for 'meaty' foods and one for 'milky' foods. Some foods are *parve*, or neutral, and can be used with either milky or meaty. It was complicated to begin with, but I soon settled into a routine, buying meat from a kosher butcher and making my own *chollah*, or sweet,

the morning. 'If he wakes screaming in the night', said the Paediatrician, 'wrap him in wet towels and put him in a plastic bin liner'. The surrealism was intensifying, but she was right. He did wake in the night, screaming, with glassy eyes and bright pink patches on his cheeks, so we did as she said and wrapped him in wet towels and a bin liner. He went back to sleep and thankfully, by the morning, his skin was cool again and he had turned the corner. Two days later he was more-or-less his normal self, playing on the steps of a great church and making 'binoculars' out of bottle-tops. We were just so grateful to God for answering prayer and healing him in those shocking and unfamiliar circumstances.

Chapter 12 : The London Years (Part Three)

Once back in England we continued to attend our local, evangelical, Anglican church and gradually Ian took a more formal role in leading services. It was suggested, therefore, that he should apply to the Diocese (of Southwark) to train as a Lay Reader. This would involve two years of part-time study and equip him for lay ministry. The call to the ordained ministry hadn't weakened, but the same concerns as before were expressed: would my past bar him from being accepted? At that time, most certainly 'yes', but he was content to wait. A real call, we felt, can withstand the test of time. We were so pleased that his application was accepted; and he completed the course and was licensed as a Lay Reader, in Southwark Cathedral, in 1993. I felt enormously proud of him and pleased for him, and marvelled at him in his new clerical robes of black cassock, white surplice and long, blue preaching scarf.

In time it became possible for me to return to Tearfund, who were very understanding of the pressures upon me and gave me flexibility in my work, for which I was very grateful. By now, rather like Cambridge University Press, our department had joined up with others in much bigger refurbished, open-plan premises, though still in Teddington. I had moved on from my earlier job and, although still working in the Home Department, I became more involved in the Prayer and Information Ministry, as well as continuing to promote the organisation through deputation and writing.

What really interested me was to put Tearfund's work within a global, socio/economic and political framework, informing our constituency of the role of local indigenous Christian organisations (with whom we worked), as they operated within the much broader context of their country's life and circumstances. The very personal experience I had gained all those years ago in Cambridge, as I prayed for those involved in the Falklands War, became very pertinent to my new situation. By this time the storms in my own prayer life had largely passed; I knew that we could bring the most desperate situations to God in prayer, and that He would always be willing to listen and to answer.

We were challenged many times by overwhelming need, often involving failed rains and famine, or the fall-out from war, or a combination of these and other factors. We developed an international prayer network called 'World Watch Prayer Link', with Prayer Posters and Information Sheets which could be pinned on church noticeboards, or used in church Intercessions, or adapted for a teaching context, or inserted in a church magazine. I was always gratified to hear from colleagues that they had seen, in some far-flung corner of the globe, pinned on a wall, a hastily-translated copy of one of our bulletins. We just wanted to get the information out there, for prayer.

And we did experience wonderful answers to those prayers – the hungry finally being fed, clothed and sheltered, the sick healed, those wrongfully imprisoned being freed, hurricanes being diverted from their destructive paths, corrupt regimes being toppled in favour of good government and wars coming to an end. It was a very challenging time, but also very rewarding, especially as we set up a Prayer Room at Tearfund and people signed up to take their turn in a rota of praying. I loved it, and felt that I had found my place in the overall ministry of the Church. I found it very difficult, therefore, when Ian was offered, and accepted, a teaching post in a venerable boarding school in Sussex called Christ's Hospital, his two-year contract at a London independent school having come to an end.

We knew of Christ's Hospital because our best man had attended it; we knew that it catered for able children who nonetheless had a 'need' to board. We discovered that It had been established in London in 1552 under the fifteen-year-old king, Edward VI, the son of Henry VIII, and that it had, in 1902, moved to its spacious present headquarters near Horsham.

So far so good, but the problem was that all teaching staff were required to live on site. This was one of the core requirements of teaching there. I was pleased for Ian, but at a loss to understand how this would fit in with my job. I saw myself as a permanent member of Tearfund, until my retirement, and yet had no clear idea of how I would accomplish that at such a distance. The situation for Jonathan, too, was complex. He had been at the German School near Petersham for two years and, though now fluent in German, he wanted at least another year there to become bilingual. So what could God be saying to us, as a family? Should we move lock, stock and barrel to Christ's Hospital? Should I leave Tearfund and Jonathan leave the German School? Or should we make a phased withdrawal?

After lengthy and difficult discussions we decided that Jonathan would stay at the German School for another year, and I would stay at Tearfund, while Ian moved to Christ's Hospital. And that's what we did; but it was a very expensive, and not a very satisfactory, option. We missed each other, and so decided that Jonathan and I would move to CH (as it is colloquially known), and let out our home, for by this time we had moved to a lovely, slightly larger, semi-detached house, also in New Malden. I would then commute each day to Teddington, with a German *au pair* caring for Jonathan and keeping his German 'up', at the same time keeping the house clean, the clothes washed and ironed, and so on. It was a brave hope, but in the event, the car journey was long and tiring, easily four hours each day, and the housework was not done as I had hoped or expected.

It was therefore arranged that I would board in London from Monday to Thursday, to ease the strain, but that didn't work either. I felt that the net was closing; that my options were being blocked, all except one, that of removing myself from Tearfund altogether, and resigning myself to a new and unknown life at CH. Like a fish that fights at the end of the line, I struggled and resisted this way forward. I wanted to do my job and I wanted to be with my family, but I knew that that was simply not possible, that the two sets of circumstances were mutually incompatible. Something had to give and finally, in May 1995, when I was fifty, with the heaviest of hearts and with no expectation of any further job satisfaction, ever, I left Tearfund and deposited myself in the big, attractive, but cold house, that was now our home at Christ's Hospital.

Act 4

1995-2016

Chapter 13 : The Christ's Hospital Years (Part One)

When I say it was cold, I don't exaggerate. During that first winter the glass in the windows cracked, as did the stone lintels surrounding them, and the seat in the outside loo. It became normal for me to put on my overcoat as part of my daily dressing, and if I really wanted to experience warmth, I would switch on the electric oven and sit as close as I could. The house had also been built in 1902 and, though spacious and elegant, with six bedrooms and three reception rooms, it had not been built to withstand rural Sussex winters, at least not without a servant or two to keep the home fires burning. Indeed, any heat that was generated would go straight up the stairwell and out through the attic windows. I often thought of the wonderful coal fire that was kept going in the Staff Common Room, and longed to sit in front of it, a cup of coffee in hand, and read the newspapers. But such premises were out-of-bounds to me, a lowly spouse. My unbidden presence there would, I felt, be seen as an act of gross insubordination. And so, apart from taking Jonathan to and from school, I would stay at home alone (our *au pair* having gone back to Germany); or I would drive into Horsham and sit in a pub which also had a roaring fire, eating the largest and lightest of cheese scones, ruminating.

The feelings which had beset me so powerfully when we arrived in Eschwege assailed me again – the sense of loneliness and isolation and alienation. This time it wasn't the language that separated me off, it was the simple fact that I didn't have a role to play. For it seemed to me that the whole campus was rather like a complex play with a large and well-versed cast. Everyone, from pupils to teachers, cleaners to gardeners, and matrons to clerical staff, everyone knew their part. It was like standing on a stage, and waiting for a cue, which never came. I knew that, I too, would have to find a role, or be condemned forever to this lonely life.

Thankfully help was at hand. I had become jumpy and tearful at home, suffering from anxiety and (mildly) depression, and I knew that, for the sake of my health and sanity, I had to do something. Therefore, when I was offered a job as a 'Middle Lady', that is, a Matron's Assistant, I took it. It involved an early start in one of the boys' boarding houses, when I would gather up the dirty linen and send it off for washing in the School's own Laundry. After that the fresh laundry needed to be sorted and redistributed to their respective owners; pants and socks every day, with a shirt and (preacher's) bands added every other day. There was also a rota for changing breeches. The famous yellow stockings (never 'socks') then needed to be paired up and darned before I left at lunch-time.

It was heavy and unrelenting work, but I was with colleagues, and I had a place in the School where I could legitimately go. Gradually my circumstances changed. Some people were very kind to me, and I became acquainted with the pupils in my House. Perhaps a year later I was invited to become a House Tutor in a girls' boarding house, which was a supervisory and pastoral role, and which also helped with my integration. The very kind Headmaster said that I could, indeed, go into Common Room, and sit by the fire, and have a coffee and read the papers, and that really was a privilege. Perhaps I wouldn't have admitted it, but I was, on a good day, beginning to enjoy myself.

Before time moved on and we reached the Millennium, two important events took place. The first was that I was invited to co-write a book on the School, which would trace its development from 1552 until the present, and also give an overview of life at School as the twenty-first century loomed. It was to be a large, illustrated, coffee-table book and it involved a great many hours of work, but it was published as the century turned and has, I understand, been well-received.

The second was that I was encouraged to apply for training, within the Diocese of Chichester, to be a Lay Reader. It was my local vicar who had recommended this course of action and, as I respected and trusted him, I felt I should take the matter forward. But one could safely predict the next step; just hours of interrogation regarding my past, both by individuals and by panels of people. I talked until my head spun and my throat (and my heart) ached but, in the end, it was worth it. I was accepted for training and, in 1997, embarked on a three-year, part-time course of study.

Like Ian, I had to attend lectures, write essays, do assignments and go on placements, but all went well, and I was finally licensed in Chichester Cathedral on 17th June 2000, a very windy day. Further study at the University of Brighton enabled me to commute this qualification into a degree in Religious Education Studies. I finally had my photo taken at my graduation ceremony, in mortarboard and academic gown, more than forty years after I had left school. I felt that the scripture had been fulfilled: 'I will restore the years that the locust has eaten' (Joel 2:25a). I didn't know it then, but that was really just the beginning of my academic journey.

One aspect of this time of study deserves special mention. I was asked, as all the students were, to keep a 'spiritual' diary, writing down each day what had happened, and how I had felt about things. I've always enjoyed writing and so this was no hardship, but it seemed rather bland and directionless, just to record things without any kind of addressee. I tried, 'Dear

ALL BY GRACE

Diary', but that didn't inspire me. And so I decided to make it a letter to 'God my Father', in the same way that I had 'written' to my natural father all those years before.

And then it flowed. It had focus and function and I found both great release in writing each night, and great joy. Indeed, I continued to do this long after I had ceased training and even now, wherever I am, I write every night before turning out the light. It is now over twenty years since I began this practice, and I can only commend it to you as one of the most pleasant and rewarding ways of maintaining the divine relationship.

Before I move on I feel it would be helpful to assess the impact that my time at CH had on my Christian journey. I was deeply impressed when I first saw the School, when I travelled down with Ian from New Malden, in the snow, for his interview. It is a purpose-built, red-brick campus, designed as an integrated community, and set in over one thousand acres of beautiful Sussex countryside. It is extremely well-appointed for all its activities, academic and extra-curricular and, though only opened in 1902, redolent with tradition. For it has a continuous history with the School in London which preceded it, also known as 'Christ's Hospital', which in turn is a derivation from its earliest title of 'Chryst His House'. When it was founded in 1552 its Charter stated that it should

Chapel. This was set out in the collegiate style, with its walls decorated with scenes from the New Testament, executed in the Arts and Crafts style by Sir Frank Brangwyn. It also had a lovely stone reredos. To preach to some nine hundred people, as the pupils settled themselves and a deep peace descended, was quite breath-taking. I can still recall the (very slack), rope handrail which led up to the pulpit, and the routine of putting on and adjusting the microphone and then, sermon delivered, of reversing the process and coming back to earth again.

But there were other services, some involving full-School Communion, when one had to hold firmly to the chalice to prevent some over-enthusiastic pupils from taking more than their proffered 'sip'. 'Services', simple and private, were also held in the boarding houses, and many adults, who lived on site, also joined together in informal acts of communion and fellowship.

The time at Christ's Hospital was also challenging in terms of our own relationship, quite simply because 'home' and 'work' seemed to have no clear boundaries. If I was busy in my little role, Ian was hugely occupied in his triple role, of being a teacher of languages (both ancient and modern), an Assistant Chaplain, and as a House Master, a role that he held for ten years. We had both a cleaner and a gardener at that time, of necessity, but we still seemed to have very little time to be together. It was during this time, and to address this issue that, in 2004, we bought a lovely old townhouse in France, in the Lot valley, as a place of escape during the summer. For - though the School was now free of its normal occupants - it was equally occupied with the summer 'lets'. We still have that house and are so pleased that it has become a regular holiday home for our family and friends.

One incident that happened at Christ's Hospital deserves mention, though it challenged my credulity at the time, and no doubt will challenge yours now. But I feel that it should be told. It concerns the School's excellent Museum. It had become my practice to work in the Museum one day a week, normally on a Thursday, when we would welcome groups of visitors to the School on what were known as Verrio Tours. These groups would be greeted in the Sports Centre and given coffee before being escorted the short distance to the Museum, which was located on the top floor of the Infirmary. A talk on the School followed, with a tour of the Museum.

Lunch, preceded by the 'march-in' with the famous Marching Band, would follow; then a tour of the School itself, before completing the day with a cream tea in Dining Hall. These days were long and full, but also very rewarding and profitable, both in PR terms, and financially.

Accordingly, when I arrived at the Museum on Thursday mornings I would make sure that all was tidy and in order, in preparation.

I had noticed, when I first visited the Museum, that a thin layer of dust lay on some of the surfaces, and that the lavatories were not as clean as they might have been. I was curious about this as CH had a large team of cleaners who were trained and well-supervised, and diligent in the execution of their duties. I therefore made discreet enquiries, which produced a surprising response. One day, I was told, a cleaner had 'seen' a young girl in an old-fashioned nightdress and, believing she had seen a ghost, had recounted her story with such verisimilitude to the other cleaners that they had refused to clean there. I was sceptical about this, but another, very senior, member of staff, also reported such a sighting. So much by way of background.

It gradually became clear to me, as I tidied up on Thursday mornings, that some things were oddly out of place. Captions would be found on the floor, and removed from the object they should have been describing; an artefact 'fell' from a high shelf to a bottom shelf, even though it was in a locked glass cabinet; a trumpet (or bugle?) which was hung horizontally by two cords, was found just hanging vertically, from one, the other having apparently been snapped, although no pressure could have been exerted on it.   And the lights flickered, as though someone was flicking a switch quickly on and off. I couldn't understand it, because we were nowhere near a busy road, where vibration brought about by heavy traffic could have been a cause: and yet I wasn't frightened by it, because I was never directly threatened in any way. But I did feel that 'mischief' of some kind was being done.

And that led me to suspect the young girl in the white night-gown. The Museum was filled with many wonderful and rare artefacts which had been curated from the School's earlier life and times; and I wondered if, somehow, these may have provided the environment, or the stimulus, for these activities. I genuinely don't know. But the Curator and I shared our concerns with the Senior Chaplain, who listened carefully, and offered to conduct a service of Compline in the Museum,   which   we   gratefully   accepted. 'Deliver us from the perils and dangers of this night', is one of the heartfelt prayers of that wonderful old liturgy, and I felt that I was, in reality, part of the eternal 'communion of saints', who knew and understood so much more than I about spiritual activity, good and evil, in the unseen realm. I now know of a certainty that we have absolutely nothing to fear; nothing can harm us if we are fully submitted to Christ, although such events are rather shocking. The activities stopped after that, and I have no reason to believe that they have resumed.

Chapter 14 : A Byzantine Interlude

It was while I was at CH that I was introduced to 'Byzantium' by a teacher of Medieval History. I had heard of the place in childhood, and used to enjoy intoning to myself, 'Byzantium, Constantinople, Istanbul', as I recounted its different names. Such commutations interest me, and I made it my business to find out more about Byzantium and its renowned Empire. In the latter years the term 'Byzantine' has taken on a pejorative edge, insinuating unnecessary detail and convoluted bureaucracy. Were such terms appropriate and justifiable, I wondered? Accordingly, I read all that I could about that Empire, and realised what a debt we in the West owe its citizens.

It is justifiably remarkable for its art and architecture, its culture and learning, its trade and military skill; but above all, it seems to me, we owe a debt of gratitude to the Byzantines for keeping the torch of Christianity alight through the so-called 'Dark Ages'. This was a time when Rome was in ruins following the barbarian invasions; and Jerusalem, following its sack by the Romans, was a mere shadow of its former glory. For, during this time, it was the Byzantines who thrashed out the great controversies regarding the Christian faith, and who, from the Emperor Justinian I, (in 527-

565 AD) onwards, and at great cost, sought to establish Christianity in the lands bordering the Eastern and Western Mediterranean and beyond. If ever the opportunity arose, I thought, I will go there and explore.

And then, in 2004, the opportunity did arise. For I was asked by some German friends, who had a home on the western coast of the 'Asian' side, if I would like to visit them. They were arranging a tour of the sites of the early Church, and would I like to join them? Without hesitating for a moment, I accepted; and spent a wonderful week in the company of Bavarian Catholic Christians, sharing meals and visiting the ancient archaeological sites. The Christian communities established in these places are the recipients of many of the Letters of the New Testament, and are given special mention in the Book of Revelation. It was only among those great crumbling ruins, and among the statues and the symbols of pagan ritual and revelry, that I began to understand the power and 'otherness' of Christianity. For it, too, is a Kingdom, but not one that needs territory or reinforcement by the state, with such lavish embellishments, to exert its authority. It is a Kingdom of the Spirit, expressed in the gifts and fruit of that Spirit, and energised by love, faith and prayer.

We would travel each day by minibus through the beautiful and mountainous Turkish countryside, stopping at various ancient

Christian sites to pray and sing 'Taizé' songs, united in our faith. Then the Catholic priest who travelled with us would suddenly unpack his two plastic carrier bags and produce vestments from one and a chalice, wine and wafers from another. And there, where we believed the early Christians would have met, we celebrated the Eucharist together. 'Drink it! Drink it!' he would say to some of his astonished celebrants, who hesitated about taking the wine; they were not used to this freedom. I agreed with him, and our Muslim German-speaking guide and driver, stood at the side, watching.

We visited the tiny and ancient house near Ephesus known as 'Meryem Ana', believed to have been the home of the Apostle John, and Mary, the mother of Jesus; and met the nuns whose small community was based there. We later took communion together on the candle-lit terrace, with our driver, to one side, still standing and watching. I was so pleased that I had persevered with my study of German, for it meant that I could talk with him about our experiences, as we ate together on the terrace of the hotel at the end of the day. This was a time of heightened enjoyment, as the cranes settled on their nests among the chimneys, and the moon hung large and bright in the night sky.

They were wonderful, heady days and I can recall still the little indicators of Christianity that were dotted among the pagan symbols: the cross, the fish and the anchor, all cryptic signs of a shared belief and, probably, of a secret meeting place.

In the October of that year I returned to Turkey, this time to Istanbul. I had developed an interest in, bordering on a preoccupation with, the great church-turned-mosque-turned-museum called St Sophia (or the Church of Holy Wisdom), which was built in the sixth century under the patronage of the Emperor Justinian I, and very much looked forward to seeing it. I also hoped to visit the vast nearby underground water cistern which had been commissioned by Justinian I, as well as the great and ancient walls and ramparts which still surround the city. And, if possible, and I could make myself understood, I wanted to see the famed mosaics in the Church of St Saviour in Chora, in the suburbs of Istanbul. I had chosen my hotel because I knew it was located near St Sophia, but nothing could have prepared me for the view I had on my first evening when a kindly waiter led me to the roof terrace and, offering me a coffee, pointed ahead.

For there she was, not more than two hundred yards away and 'pinker' than I had realised, the great mother church, with her domes and buttresses and minarets. I was only in Istanbul for five days, but I loved it, and visited St Sophia each day, trying to commit to memory the rare splendour of its vast interior. It has lost a lot of its earlier marble and gilding, but it is still breathtakingly beautiful and impressive. I tried to picture it when it was in full use as a centre of Christian worship, with oil-lamps, and candles, with rare incense; and massed choirs and teams of priests. I tried to visualise the procession and veneration of the icons; and imagine the great sung liturgies, with successive Emperors, resplendent in silks, gold and precious stones, leading the worship alongside the Patriarch. The great image of the Virgin depicted in the dome would have looked down on all of it.

I was pleased that I was able to join a tour of the Topkapi Palace. And I spent over an hour in the Basilican Cistern, the wonderful and vast underground reservoir which, supported by rows of ancient classical columns, now has walkways, and has been very tastefully enriched by mood lighting and music. And I was able to communicate sufficiently with the hotel staff to arrange for a car and a driver to take me to the Church of St Saviour in Chora. It is fairly traditional from the outside, and its location is unremarkable; but inside it is a treasure-house of the mosaicists' craft. Scenes from the New Testament are depicted around the walls with astonishing delicacy and skill and then suddenly, looking up to a domed ceiling, one is confronted by an image of Jesus rarely seen in the West, that of the *Pantokrator*, or 'Ruler of the World'.

It is a stern and almost frightening depiction, but

I believe it to be more accurate, much more, than the rather sanitised and gentilised images that are frequently used to represent Him in the West. My driver spoke little English, and that mostly of the 'No problem!' variety, but he did understand my request that we drive past the great city walls which border the Bosphorus on our homeward journey. They are ancient and massive, with their ramparts and triple defence-mechanisms; and one can only admire the skill of their builders and the courage of those who manned them, particularly on 29th May 1453, the day that the great city of Constantinople finally fell to its Ottoman neighbours and enemies.

My faith was certainly enriched by this brief immersion into the Byzantine interpretation of Christianity, and I was delighted when, in 2016, the Ashmolean Museum in Oxford mounted a major exhibition entitled, *Sicily and the Sea*, and included artefacts which attest to the role played by 'Byzantium' in the building of churches and the spread of the faith in the West. It is a story which deserves re-telling in each generation, and I am so grateful that circumstances allowed me to participate in it in this entirely pleasant way.

After my return I was able to continue my links with 'Byzantium' by, occasionally, attending the Orthodox Church in Oxford. At that time I had no idea that I would study Archaeology in Oxford but, in due course, and as my studies progressed, I was invited to develop links with the wonderful Centre for Late Antique and Byzantine Studies, in St Giles. And I was so pleased when, as part of my Post-Graduate Certificate in 2012, and with the support of the Ashmolean Museum, I was able to base my dissertation on a study of Byzantine coins, found in Britain, which had been minted since 498 AD. There are well over one hundred, mostly found by metal detectorists, and indicate a level of trade and exchange much greater than had been presumed. It would be good to work further on this interesting topic.

Chapter 15: The Christ's Hospital Years (Part Two)

One of the major decisions we had made when we relocated to Christ's Hospital was that Jonathan should attend the local primary school for the next three years, until he took the Christ's Hospital Entrance Exam, because it was a good school and it was also state-funded. We were helping to support my daughter financially now that she was at university, and two sets of fees would have been punitive. But Jonathan flourished under his new circumstances and passed the exam, joining CH in 1998, at the age of eleven. He did well and eventually, in 2005, secured a Choral Scholarship at New College, Oxford, (for he too has a wonderful bass voice), where he would sing in the famous Choir, and read Classics for four years.

We were naturally very pleased for him, but with his departure to embark on this new lifestyle, some of my earlier trials came back to distress me. While he had been at home the house had always been filled with fun and laughter, with friends and with music, for he played a variety of instruments and was always rehearsing for some performance or other. Suddenly the big Housemaster's house in which we lived seemed quiet and empty. Too quiet. Too empty.

I had become used to a kitchen full of senior pupils like himself who, in their elegant 'Housey' Coats, would sit at the kitchen table, consuming mountains of toast and drinking tea. Suddenly, like a flock of birds, they had migrated to various universities, and the kitchen was empty. I tried to throw myself deeper into the life of the School, but I knew that, inside, I was grieving. I understand now, as I didn't before, how real and serious the 'empty nest syndrome' is. But I didn't suffer in silence and try to put a brave face on it. I shared my feelings with Ian and Jonathan and they felt I should engage in some kind of study, something which would really interest and occupy me. So good, but what?

It was while we were visiting Jonathan (now called 'Johnny' by his friends) in Oxford that enlightenment came, as we sat together in the Ashmolean Museum coffee shop. For on the table was a leaflet advertising a part-time undergraduate course in Archaeology, to be taken over five years, and based in Rewley House, which is the Department for Continuing Education (under the aegis of the University of Oxford), in Wellington Square, just off Little Clarendon Street. I just knew that that was what I wanted to do, and so applied, and was accepted, and began my studies in 2007, after we had bought a little flat in Great Clarendon Street, to act as my base and to be our bolt-hole in Oxford.

Before I move on I feel that I should mention an unusual situation which occurred during these Christ's Hospital years. It relates to a rather good oil painting on wood, signed and dated, and depicting a beautiful walled garden, which I had purchased at auction in Kingston in 1978, as part of a job-lot for my shop. The painting showed smooth lawns with deep and mature herbaceous borders and a wonderful array of flowering plants and shrubs. The 'walls' which bordered the garden on one side looked old, and were very high and deep with an unusual seat set into what looked like ramparts. It was mounted in an attractive, and original, Edwardian, gilt frame; and the back was covered over by brown paper.

I had no idea of the location of its subject. Anyway, I just liked it, and so I kept it and it was either hung in various locations or stored away until after Johnny was born in 1987, when it was hung outside his bedroom.

One day, and I still don't know why, sometime between 2005-9, when Johnny was at New College, the paper on the back came off and the writing on the wood declared that it was 'The Walled Garden at New College, Oxford'. Those 'walls' were the ancient and famous walls of the medieval town of Oxford, sections of which are contiguous with the buildings of New College. I had very often walked passed them, on my way to and from Chapel, and strolled in those gardens, and sat in the seat set into the ramparts. Now that I find remarkable.

Chapter 16 : The Oxford Years

These were heady times indeed! To withdraw, if only briefly, from the insularity of CH to the cosmopolitan atmosphere of Oxford was very stimulating and, to my surprise and delight, Johnny and I met up each day, or as often as possible. Sometimes only for the briefest time, but I always felt better for meeting him. I would frequently go to New College Chapel for the wonderful services of Choral Evensong or Eucharist, and always felt enriched and inspired by that place of worship and its beautiful singing. He sang in the choir for six days out of seven, and that regular and intense dedication to his craft, under the hand of an inspirational choir-master, turned him into a singer of some stature. He now spends at least seven months of each year travelling the world as a member of a world-famous six-man *a capella* group, performing in venues large and small, and singing for his supper.

And I was busy with my studies, working hard and making new friends. I learnt so much from that time, as I completed first the Certificate, then the Diploma and finally the Post-Graduate Certificate, in Archaeology. Now I'm an Associate Alumnus of Oxford University, which entitles me to a small discount on coffee and other refreshments, as well as on books. At first I only stayed in the flat as often as I needed, just two or three days a week, but gradually the pattern changed as I needed greater access to the libraries and had weekend activities. Ian would come up as often as he could, and I loved it when he arrived very early on Saturday mornings, having beaten the traffic, knowing that we could have a whole weekend together. We only sold the flat last year, when I finally accepted that I could no longer climb the twenty-one external steps to our front-door, even without the shopping. Johnny lived there for a short while, but he has now moved to London.

After Johnny left New College in 2009, and when I was no longer active in the Chaplaincy Team at CH, I wondered where I could serve as a Lay Reader. I put out feelers in Oxford and was told that the Dean of Chapel at New College would welcome some assistance. Accordingly we met and settled things between us. My 'transfer' to the Diocese of Oxford was quickly completed and, for four years, from 2012-16, I was the Licensed Lay Minister at New College. Nothing in all of my life could have prepared me for this honour. I thank God for it and will never forget it: the singing and the choristers and their parents, the dark candle-lit interior; the wonderful public performances of masses and *oratoria*, the jokes and camaraderie in the Vestry, the slight trace of junior testosterone as I walked through The Song Room (the choristers' practice room), past the high, graffiti-covered, desks, with mortar-boards askew and duffle coats fallen on the floor; as well as the simple times of prayer and quiet reflection. I served there on Sundays and Thursdays, and loved it.

Ian, meanwhile, could not ignore the call to ordination, which gently but firmly persisted. To clarify matters he met, in 2007, with the local Diocesan Director of Ordinands for the Diocese of Chichester, who suggested that he, Ian, press the door, gently, to see what would happen. He would have to submit to a wide-ranging and in-depth, two-year 'discernment process', which would test his calling and suitability for the ordained ministry.

So far so good, but would my past continue to be a bar to his ordination? There was only one way to find out. For it transpired that his application would only be considered if I was willing to submit to a process called a C4 Panel.

Of course I was and, challenging and painful as it was, I seem to have satisfied my many inquisitors, for he was finally allowed, in 2009, to put his name forward for the formal selection process called a BAP, or Bishop's Advisory Panel.

Screeds could be written about the following months and years, but they would serve little purpose. For reasons never explained to us, Ian was 'not recommended' by two selection panels, but he was, whole-heartedly and without reservation, by the third. And so he finally began a three-year part-time training course for the Anglican ministry, based at Southwark, in 2013; and was ordained 'deacon' in Christ Church Cathedral in Oxford, in July 2016, having been transferred from the Diocese of Chichester to the Diocese of Oxford. He was then appointed to serve as Curate at a joint living just west of Oxford, at St John's Church in Carterton, with St Britius Church in Brize Norton.

He was finally ordained 'priest' in June 2017, at wonderful old Dorchester Abbey, just outside Oxford, and is now able to take a full part – leading services, presiding over Holy Communion, as well as blessing, absolving, baptising, joining in marriage and burying folk – in the spiritual life of the community. He also works, for two days a week, at a local Independent co-educational school, as a teacher of German and as the School Chaplain. He loves it and people love him.

We live in a large, modern, four-bedroomed house owned by the Diocese of Oxford which is located in a pleasant estate nearby. It was a 'big' and exhausting move, taking possessions from the Oxford flat as well as from CH but, thankfully, we have a large double garage which, for the moment, is accommodating all our clutter. We have promised each other that we must clear it in the next two years.

We haven't 'left' Oxford. It is only fourteen miles away, to the east of us, and we are frequent visitors there, but that particular phase of our lives has come to an end. Ian left Christ's Hospital in July 2016, after twenty-two years of distinguished service, and we are so grateful that, during this time, our little flat in Oxford enabled us both to live rich and fulfilling lives, much of it in company with Johnny, for over ten years.

Act 5

2016-2018

(and incorporating events from 2010-14)

Chapter 17 : Vienna, my Health, and becoming a Curate's Wife

One city which we visited both regularly and frequently was Vienna, the home-town of Ian's mother and grandmother and, indeed, the seat of his family following the break-up of the Austro-Hungarian Empire at the end of the First World War. Ian still has non-Jewish relatives there and initially, when we first visited that great city in about 1984, we stayed with them. The recollection of opening the window of our bedroom on the first morning, and hearing cars and trams 'rattle' along the cobbled streets, will always remain with me. I felt almost euphoric to be there; I felt that even the air was different and, though I spoke very little German at the time, I knew that I wanted this contact with Vienna to be a permanent feature of my life.

And so it has transpired. I have visited the city, and Ian's relations, alone, or with Ian for over thirty years, and every time I thank God for the opportunity afforded me. I now stay in a simple, ancient, Benedictine guest-house, right in the centre by the old city walls, and have coffee shops, restaurants, and shops of all kinds nearby. Over the years we have visited the great museums, churches and libraries and would say, with a right modesty, I hope, that we know Vienna quite well. I am so grateful that we were able to go there again this summer, and meet up with friends and relations. I just needed additional oxygen on the plane, as well as a wheelchair to get about; I simply don't know if that will be my last visit.

My visit of 2010 is important, for it was then that I had my accident. It had been a very cold week in Vienna, with temperatures falling to well below freezing and with lots of snow, which I love. On my last day, in the week before Christmas, it snowed all day, and so I stayed in the guest-house and read in a desultory manner while, all the time, watching the snow as it settled outside the window. I became a little anxious when the taxi I had ordered to take me to the airport was late, and then panicked slightly when he finally did arrive and phoned Reception. He had apparently arrived on time, but was unable to park properly because people had abandoned their cars (mostly due to a surfeit of *Glühwein*, but also because of the snow), and could I make my own way to him? I put on my coat, and gathered my bags, and made my way to the lift. As the lift-door opened I picked up my heavy suitcase and, as I did so, there was a tremendous 'crack' which reverberated up and down the lift-shaft, and the suitcase fell from my lifeless fingers. My arm, like a broken crane, hung uselessly by my side. At the same time intense pains shot up my back and around my ribs.

At first I couldn't understand what had

happened. Where had that sound come from? Only later did I understand that it was the dreadful sound of some of my vertebrae and ribs fracturing. I kicked the suitcase into the lift, then down to the pavement and across to the waiting taxi, where the driver put it in the boot. Thankfully a wheelchair had been ordered for me at the airport, which meant that I was in receipt of 'Special Assistance'. How grateful I was! My baggage was 'dropped' as a priority, and I stayed in that blessed wheelchair until my flight was finally called, many hours later, once Gatwick had given the assurance that the plane could land there, for it too, was frozen and covered in snow. Finally I arrived home and went straight to bed, where I stayed for all of Christmas and for some time after, in acute pain. Nothing surgically could be done. I just had to wait for the passage of time and pray that God would heal me. And so began a train of events which had grave consequences, which are affecting me still.

It would be lovely to be able to say that God graciously healed me of this accident, but that is not quite the case. The spinal column has healed, as far as medical science can tell, but in the process my spine has twisted into an 'S' shape, and turned sideways, in a condition known as kyphoscoliosis, such as Richard III had.

Dependency on steroids over the years, of

necessity prescribed for my asthma, has led to osteoporosis, and this in turn has led to the weakness in my spine. I don't have a hump-back, but I am some five inches shorter than I used to be, and in pain for a lot of the time, as muscles have had to take the place of bones in holding up my back and head. And the pain hasn't just been physical: it has also 'pained' me not to be tall, as I used to be. I enjoyed being tall and having a certain 'style', and after the accident I thought, 'What's the point? Nothing will ever look good again!' It has taken me some time to come to terms with this new situation, and to find a certain peace and acceptance within it. In truth, my vanity has taken as much of a blow as my back, and is proving just as hard to heal.

In 2014 my health took another hit, a double-hit, in fact, as I had pneumonia (with meningitis B, pleurisy and sepsis) in April, and then had a heart attack in October. For both of these conditions I received the very best care and, from each, made a good recovery; but the consequences, more spiritual than physical, stayed with me for some time. For shortly after my heart attack I underwent a procedure called an 'angiogram', and it was in the course of that that I had a cardiac arrest. I remember a hooter going off and people calling, 'Crash team! Crash team!', and then nothing further until I woke in a hospital bed and saw a nurse. I recall that I commended myself into God's care as I 'slipped away', not knowing where I would wake up. When I saw the nurse, and felt the cool sheets next to my skin, I was so relieved to know that I was still 'here', still with my family and living to fight another day. I am deeply grateful to those who worked so hard to resuscitate me.

It took me a while to recover from this incident, and when I did, many questions were swirling round in my head. Why hadn't I been transported to some heavenly landscape, as I understood had been the experience of others? What was death? Had I actually 'died', although I had had no pulse or heartbeat? Was I ready to die? What did my faith tell me about death and the afterlife? At first I kept such thoughts to myself, but finally had to admit that I was struggling and asked Ian for help. And it was at that point that we came into contact with the Cambridge Institute for Orthodox Christian Studies, and saw that they were offering an on-line two-year Certificate which included a module entitled, 'Mysteries of Life and Death'.

This sounded exactly what I needed. There was no hushing up of the matter of death, or skirting around it as a morbid and taboo subject. This was a serious examination of the role of faith and obedience in the Christian journey; a journey which, according to Eastern Orthodox tradition, goes seamlessly through the final frontier and into the courts of heaven itself. I was convinced that this would help me, and enrolled on the course in 2015 and finished in August 2017, completing my final essay, being cooled by a fan, in the heat of a French summer. And I haven't been disappointed, because the information I discovered has helped me, as we have made preparations for this new phase in our lives, to have 'certainty' and assurance in areas of former confusion and 'mystery'. It is to an examination of those discoveries that I will now turn.

Chapter 18 : Life, Death and the Homeward Journey

Probably the greatest impact my studies had on me was the realisation that my 'salvation' wasn't something that just applied to *this lifetime*; that it only availed to forgive my sins and receive, as a free gift, the righteousness of Christ in place of my sinfulness. I understood, as I simply had not seen before, that my salvation also availed at the time of my departure *from* this life. That, rather than be subject to some divine lottery, I could have absolute assurance that – because of Jesus' death in full payment for my sins - I would go to heaven; and that I would enjoy the 'communion of the saints', and understand all mysteries, and come into the presence of Love Himself. Suddenly I 'knew' that; I didn't have to worry or speculate any more.

And then I understood that, when we take the step of repentance and receive forgiveness, we are transported from the kingdom of evil or 'darkness', into the kingdom of righteousness, or 'light' (Colossians 1:12-13). That there are, in fact, two parallel kingdoms: we are born into the 'bad' one, (even though we don't know it), and our lives are subject to the rules and rulers of that kingdom, unless their power over us is mitigated by the prayers of other believers. I am convinced that it was the prayers of my parents which enabled me to 'repent and believe', otherwise I might still be trapped in the consequences of my transgressions.

Jesus said that it was for this reason He had come into the world, to proclaim the Kingdom of God (Matthew 4:23); and I realised that it was now the central task of each believer to extend that Kingdom; through prayer of all kinds, through performing 'good works', and through the faithful proclamation of the gospel. I suddenly saw, as I hadn't seen before, what my 'job description' was: to give expression to these three commands, as God directed. That understanding both calmed and challenged me. What was I doing to fulfil these commands and, whatever it was, was it enough?

And I realised that the difficult matter of 'suffering' lay within the remit of this understanding: that it was the evil kingdom which was responsible for most of the misery and suffering in the world, for Satan only wants 'to steal, kill and destroy', whereas God wants us 'to have life, in all its fullness' (John 10:10). I add the word, 'mostly' as a caveat, for there are clearly instances where wonderful Christian people do suffer, and one simply cannot explain the cause. I believe we must accept that there is an element of mystery which most people cannot explain: the Apostle Paul alludes to this in his great discourse on 'love', to the believers in Corinth, in which he says that, 'if I have the gift of prophecy *and can fathom all mysteries* and all knowledge, and if I have a faith that can move mountains, but have not love, I am nothing.' (1 Corinthians 13: 1-2).

From my studies I understood that I stand in possession of a great spiritual legacy, which was laid down by the Patriarchs of the Old Testament, and continued through the Prophets, and found its greatest revelation in Jesus, and was given further illumination by the Disciples and the Apostles and the Church Fathers, and is still being given clarification by wise and humble believers today.

This is the Body of Christ and I am a member of that Body, and I will take my place in the unfolding revelation of that story. It was an exhilarating moment when I 'saw' myself as part of a Body which exists in both Time and Eternity: until that moment I had really only 'seen' myself as part of Christ's Body on earth, reflected in the past and the present, and not as a precious member of the Bride of Christ, existing fully and gloriously in the future, in heaven.

Further understanding came when I had to study the 'ascent into holiness', one of the great themes of Eastern Orthodoxy. Drawing on the experience of Saints such as St Anthony, the first of the Desert Fathers, and St John Climacus in his 'Ladder of Divine Ascent', I began to understand that we, as believers in Jesus, are all on a path to holiness which, through trials, obedience, good works, and the application of faith and the practice of prayer, will lead us to the courts of heaven and, ultimately, to our *deification*, or union with God. For, according to Orthodox belief, it is one continuous journey, and one that death does not interrupt. For the moment of death is swift and our translation immediate. There is no 'me' lying in a coffin or mouldering in a cold grave, only the empty vessel that supported 'me'.

These were some of the answers that came to me as I tried to come to terms with death, a process made ever-more pressing because so many medical people asked me at what point I wanted, or did not want, to be resuscitated. We were clear ourselves on the matter: I didn't want to prolong life if it meant I would be a burden to others, or would be in a vegetative state. Beyond that I could not say, but felt that I must trust to the wisdom and skill of medical staff and to the mercy of God. But at last I was at peace: I had finally confronted my fears about death and knew, of a certainty, that I had absolutely nothing to fear. I just needed to live each day in repentance and faith, trusting in God for the rest.

It was difficult leaving the flat in Jericho, and it was hard to leave Christ's Hospital. We had been happy in both places, and the future was unknown. I had never been to Carterton; indeed, I thought anything outside of Oxford itself was alien and foreign. But move we must, and on 12th and 13th July 2016, we left Christ's Hospital and Jericho, and moved into our present house. It was a fresh and windy day and, as I sat in the hall and directed the removal men, I felt cold and sad. But they were wonderful, knowing far better than we, where items of furniture should go.

The congregations at both churches have welcomed us warmly and we have only known kindness and support since we have been here. Ian is very busy with his triple role of Curate, Chaplain and Clerk to the Governors of the local Church of England Primary School; but we have time to go to the new Costa coffee shop in the town, and to shop at Morrisons, or to go to the neighbouring towns of Witney or Burford for a greater range of goods. Or to meet up with Jonathan, when his schedule permits, or with my daughter and her husband, and their three wonderful children.

My wheezes are now so much better than they used to be, and only really trouble me if I have a chest infection. But my lungs have taken such a battering over the years that they are now only able to work at less than a third of their capacity. I get very breathless and can only walk about twenty or thirty yards unaided, but I have a New Best Friend in a mobility scooter, which is a dream and takes me, uncomplaining, almost anywhere, but not very fast.

I have to be on oxygen at home for fifteen hours a day, and I am aware that my heart and lungs are struggling to meet the demands made daily upon them. But there are also compensations. We have acquired Jonathan's BMW, a handsome and sporty beast, which is both comfortable and fast, and was wonderful for the long drive through France last summer. I now have a new computer and, free of the constraints of my studies, I find great pleasure simply in 'writing'. I have made the decision that the only way I can cope with the frustrations and convolutions of Brexit and other political activities is to pray about them, and to write letters to influential people or departments in Government, and that brings great release. Without prayer and the certain knowledge of a wise and loving and all-powerful God, I think one would just go mad.

As I conclude I must report that, in the last few days, certain events have taken place which could cause me to write differently about my health. Many people have prayed for and with me for my healing over the years, but there has never been any spectacular breakthrough. I assumed, therefore, that it wasn't within the purposes of God to heal me at this stage. However, two weeks ago we had a 'Healing Service' at church during which two members of the congregation laid hands on me, and I wondered if this might be God's 'time' to restore me. Nothing happened at the time and I returned to my seat, but the following Sunday I started to have some sensation under my left foot. I must explain that, for almost a year, I had had almost no feeling in either of my feet; now I could feel a big muscle under my left foot 'pulling' as I walked. I could hardly believe it.

It did actually rather hurt, but I didn't care about the pain. I was just so thrilled that some 'process' was at work. I now have feeling in both my feet, and can feel other muscles 'pulling' as the Achilles' tendon links up with, and activates, my calf muscles. I feel like a child, having to learn to walk again, but I am in awe of what has happened in the last few weeks. I have the hope within me that this is just the beginning of a complex and lengthy process and, if I'm right, I will set it out in print. For it will be nothing less than a series of miracles.

I chose the title, 'All by Grace', for this book long before I began to write it. Grace has been described by someone who clearly liked using such literary devices as, God's Riches at Christ's Expense, which is a clever acronym. Grace is extremely difficult to describe, for it can only be seen through the lens of some kind of activity; it does not exist in a vacuum, or stand alone. It is a medium through which other activity takes place, giving it value and effectiveness and success. It also has connotations of controlled power, and self-giving love, and purity and beauty. It is discernible in its presence and in its absence. When I recall the Marxist gatherings I attended all those years ago, I can say that they were 'grace-less'; there was no evidence of any of the attributes which I have listed above. There was a kind of comradeship, but it lacked any love or warmth or the mutual honouring which characterises truly Christ-like activity. Grace is like the divine unction, or holy oil, which moves between component parts and enables God's purposes to be accomplished.

It was by grace that I was able to withstand the shocks and trials of my childhood. It was by grace that I was able to get jobs, and accommodation, and enjoy good and loving relationships. It was by grace that I was able to cope with the separation from my daughter and recover from the miscarriage. It was by grace that I have been able to travel and learn new languages and value my 'European' heritage. It is by grace that I have two wonderful children and a loving and supportive family. It was by grace that I was able to study, both for theological training, and then in Archaeology; and it was by grace that I had memorable years in both Cambridge and Oxford, as well as in London, Germany and Christ's Hospital.

It was by grace that my mother was able to walk the steep and narrow path of obedience and love, finally dying peacefully in her hospital chair on Christmas Eve, 1992, at the age of 84. It is by grace poured out on a daily, even hourly measure, that I am able to cope with the trials and frustrations of my present physical infirmities. It was by grace that I met and married Ian. It is by grace that the inner chambers of my grief are now empty and redundant. But, more than these, it was Grace Himself who reached down and drew me up, when I was in real danger of falling into the mire of human misery and sin. It was grace that gave me hope. It was grace that enabled me to forgive. It was grace that enabled me to give and to receive love.

It was the grace of God that drew me back to church and gave me a new understanding of my Christian faith. It was grace that enabled me to repent of my sins and receive the riches of God's forgiveness. It was by grace that I received the gift of the Holy Spirit and entered into a wholly new experience of prayer and revelation. It was by grace that I knew I was loved by God, and 'accepted in the beloved', when I so feared the pain of rejection. It was by grace that I was able to accept and rejoice in the mysteries of the Christian faith - the Virgin Birth, the death, burial, Resurrection and the Ascension of Jesus - as well as the miracles which He and His followers performed. It is by grace that I have the firm assurance of eternal life and a firm hope in a joyful union with the Godhead. 'It is by grace you have been saved, through faith – and this is not of yourselves, it is the gift of God - not by works, so that no-one can boast', as the Apostle Paul tells the believers in Ephesus,

(Ephesians 2:8-9). It is all by grace.

I am now seventy-three, and able to do so much less now than I used to; but Ian has responded with grace to our new situation and does most of what is needed, and always with humour and a light touch. We have been married for thirty-seven years, and it is forty years since he first heard the 'call' to the ordained ministry, but I believe now that it was worth the wait. I'm sure his experiences as a teacher, Housemaster, father and husband, will continue to enrich his ministry. My daughter is now forty-three, a radiant Christian and a wise and loving wife, mother, sister and daughter. We are still in good contact with her father and his partner, and I am so grateful for their goodwill and kindness in many difficult circumstances over the years, not least in the support of Ian's ordination. We have no idea what the future holds; we try to make the most of each day and to trust God for the rest.

I said at the outset that my intention was to explain why I was a Christian, and what those beliefs mean to me. I hope I have succeeded. My desire is that some part of my story will chime with yours. That there is something about the way God has dealt with me that will prompt you to call on Him as I have done. For He will hear you, and He will answer. 'Come unto me', (He will say), 'all you who are weary and burdened, and I will give you rest. Take my yoke upon you and learn from me; for I am gentle and humble in heart and you will find rest for your souls. For my yoke is easy and my burden is light.' (Matthew 11:28-30). That is my deepest and heartfelt prayer for you: that you, too, will call upon the grace and mercy of God, and in doing so, you will find lasting peace, joy and satisfaction.

Postscript
A Suggested Prayer

If you want to make such a prayer, but are not sure how to say it, here is a suggested format. It can, of course, be amended to suit your particular circumstances.

Dear Loving Heavenly Father,

I come before you now as a sinner who is in need of forgiveness. I confess my sins and deeply regret them, and repent of them, and ask you to forgive me for them. I acknowledge that, when Jesus died on the cross, He took the guilt and just punishment for those sins, and I receive His forgiveness as a free gift. I believe that His death was the death of 'the old me', and that He rose again on the third day to give me new life.

Please help me to think and live in a new way, being guided by your Holy Spirit; and, through the words of the Bible, and in fellowship with other believers, to do more and more what is right and pleases you. Please guide me each day in what I should do, and give me the wisdom and grace I need to live a life which serves and honours You, and helps my neighbour.

Please lead me to a church where I can both contribute as a Christian, and grow in my understanding of my Christian faith. Please fill me with your Holy Spirit, and help me to display the fruit of that Spirit in my life. Please help me to be a channel of your peace, grace and love, and to become ever-more Christ-like as my spiritual journey unfolds.

In the name of Jesus, my Saviour,

AMEN

(Prayer written by Rosie Howard)

Appendix

A Very Short History of Jesus and an Explanation of the Gospel He Proclaimed.

It is being impressed upon me that, as I have written about the 'work' which Jesus accomplished, I should also introduce Him to you, as you may have heard about Him, but know little of His life and work. He was a Jewish man born sometime between 6 BCE and 2 BCE. This calculation depends partially on the date of the death of Herod the Great, and also on certain stellar and planetary phenomena, which might be interpreted as 'the star of Bethlehem', which the 'wise men saw in the East' (Matthew 2:2, 9, 10.). His mother was a thoughtful and intelligent young Jewish woman called Mary and his father was an older man, (or so it was thought) also a Jew, called Joseph, a carpenter.

They lived in the northern city of Nazareth, in the land of Israel, but Jesus was actually born in Bethlehem, in the south, an event depicted in Nativity Plays and celebrated at Christmas. At some point His mother Mary tells the evangelist Luke that an angel called Gabriel visited her, and told her that she would become pregnant with a son, and that the father would be God Himself. This event is known as 'the Virgin Birth'. Nothing is known of Jesus' appearance, and little is known of His childhood except that, even at the age of twelve, he was an accomplished rabbinic scholar. It is probable that He also trained as a carpenter and was bilingual in Aramaic and Hebrew.

It is only when he reaches the age of about thirty, and begins his public ministry, that the gospel-writers tell us a great deal more about His life and work. For three intense years He travelled up and down the land of Israel, which was by then under Roman occupation, and performed many miracles. These included miracles of healing, and of casting out evil spirits, as well as raising the dead. Great crowds followed Him and He, through parables as well as through 'direct' teaching and preaching, proclaimed 'the Kingdom of God'. At the beginning of these three years He was baptised by his cousin John ('the Baptist') in the river Jordan, and it is from this point onwards that it is made clear that His actual Father was, indeed, God Himself.

Jesus is, therefore, 'the Son of God', a title which is often used of Him. He frequently calls Himself 'the Son of Man', indicating His dual nature: being both fully human and fully divine (as referred to in Daniel 7:13). He also tacitly acknowledged Himself to be the long-awaited Messiah of the Jewish people, hence His other name of 'Christ'. Both words mean 'the Anointed One'. After three years of public ministry He was charged with blasphemy by the

Jewish religious leaders, with whom He had long-standing and heated disagreements, and was sentenced to death. He was crucified just outside Jerusalem – a shameful and painful Roman punishment – and His lifeless body was brought down from the cross and placed in a new, empty, rock-cut, tomb, which was then securely sealed.

However, three days later, when the women went to the tomb to embalm His body, they found that it was empty, the great stone which had been used to 'seal' it, having been rolled aside. This is called 'the Resurrection'.

But Jesus was still here on earth and appeared to His disciples and many others before being taken back up to heaven forty days later, in an event known as the Ascension. During this time, between the Resurrection and the Ascension, His body appears to have changed and to have acquired new properties: He could still eat and drink and speak and walk in the same way, but He could also go through walls and appear and disappear at will.

He is now in heaven, at the right-hand of God the Father, and is making continual intercession for His people, the believers, on earth. But the Holy Spirit, the third Person of the Godhead, was sent dramatically as wind and fire, ten days after the Ascension, to empower the believers on earth. And it is in the power of that Spirit that we are enabled to live the Christian life. These central events in the life of Jesus – the Virgin Birth, the Resurrection, and the Ascension – are impossible to explain from a human point of view: they are quite outside our sphere of rational thought and understanding. Each person who wants to explore Christianity must form their own understanding of these events. I am grateful that I don't struggle with them as many do: I am content to accept them just as they are presented.

For further reading on this subject may I recommend:

Fields, D., & Kohlenberger J. R. III, (1998), 2007, *The one-minute Bible for students*. pub. Broadman and Holman, Nashville, Tennessee, USA. (The 366 daily 1-minute Bible Readings cover all the main teachings of the Christian faith.)

Gumbel, Nicky, (1993), 2016, *Questions of Life*, pub. Alpha International, London, SW7 1JA.

Gumbel, Nicky, (1994), 2015, *Searching Issues*, pub. Alpha International, London, SW7 1JA.

Lewis, C. S., (1942), 2002, *Mere Christianity*, pub. Harper-Collins, London, W6 8JB.

Nee, Watchman, (1957), 1961, *The Normal Christian Life*, pub. David C. Cook, Kingsway Communications Ltd, BN23 6NT.

Stott, J., (1958), 2004, *Basic Christianity*, pub. Inter-Varsity Press, Leicester, LE1 7GP.

Urquhart, Colin, (1974), 1982, *When the Spirit Comes*, pub. Hodder & Stoughton, London, EC4Y 0DZ.

Ware, T., (1963), 1997, *The Orthodox Church*, pub. Penguin Books, London. W8 5TZ.

Williams, P., & Cooper, B., 2007, *If you could ask God one question*, pub. The Good Book Company, New Malden, Surrey, KT3 3HB.

Williams, P., & Cooper, B., 2011, *One Life, What's it all about?*, pub. The Good Book Company, New Malden, Surrey, KT3 3HB.

DVDs

The Gospel of John, (2003), ChristianVideos.co.uk in association with NPN VIDEOS. Running time 180 minutes.

The Gospel of Mark, (2014), produced by The Lumo Project, in association with Toy Gun Films Inc. and Big Book Media Production. Running time 102 minutes.

Catalogue to the exhibition: *Sicily and the Sea*, published by W Books, as a joint publication between the Allard Pierson Museum, Amsterdam, and The Soprintendenza del Mare in Palermo, in co-operation with the Zenobia Foundation. The exhibition was held at the Ashmolean Museum, Oxford, from 16th June to 25th September 2016. (This Catalogue is mentioned in Chapter 14, 'A Byzantine Interlude').

Printed in Great Britain
by Amazon